Alvar Aalto

Alvar Aalto

by Karl Fleig

PRAEGER PUBLISHERS

New York · Washington

Published in the United States of America in 1975
by Praeger Publishers, Inc., 111 Fourth Avenue,
New York, N. Y. 10003

© 1974 Artemis Verlag und Verlag für Architektur, Zürich

Library of Congress Cataloging in Publication Data

Fleig, Karl, Architekt.
    Alvar Aalto.

    (Studiopaperback)
    Includes index.
    1. Aalto, Alvar, 1898—
NA1455.F53A239   720'.92'4   74—5568
ISBN 0—275—49660—0
ISBN 0—275—63610—0 pbk.

Printed in Switzerland

Table of Contents

In some cases an individual building forming part of a larger group or complex, or one constructed at a different time, may be found listed separately under the appropriate building type.

Churches

Family Houses

Apartment Blocks and High-Rise Buildings

Furniture

Urban Design

Civic Centre, Seinäjoki
Church: Competition 1952   Built 1958—1960
Centre: Competition 1959
Town hall: Designed 1961/62   Built 1963—1965
Library: Designed 1963   Built 1964/65
Parish hall: Designed 1963   Built 1964—1966
Theatre: Designed 1968/69

Two competitions were held: one, for the religious centre, in 1952; the second, for the administrative and cultural centre, in 1959. A guiding principle was the separation of motor and pedestrian traffic. The square in front of the church is designed in such a way that it can serve as an extension of the church. The second square, flanked by the town hall, library and theatre, is designed as a meeting place for the townspeople. Part of this square would be built up to form a terrace, using excavated earth from the site.

Model

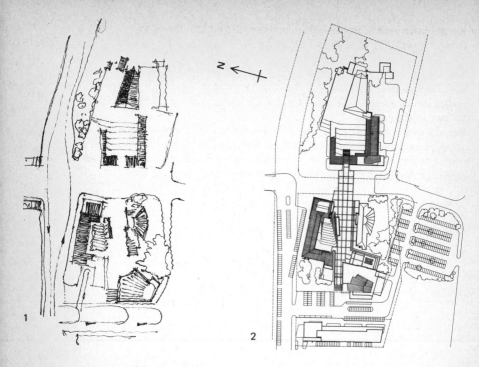

1 Site plan of the centre: first sketch
2 Site plan of the centre
3 Town hall with courtyard, staircase and church

Kampementsbacken Housing Development, Stockholm (Sweden)
Competition 1958   1st Prize   Not built

This development was intended for a site to the north of the city, on the edge of a park facing a large meadow.
Forms similar to those developed in the Berlin Hansaviertel project (1957) were to be used in the design.
Because of the nature of the site, all vehicular traffic as well as driveways and garages could be placed on the north side, about 10—20 ft below the level of the dwellings and landscaped areas. In this way undisturbed living areas with landscaped grounds and children's play spaces could be provided.

Sketch plan

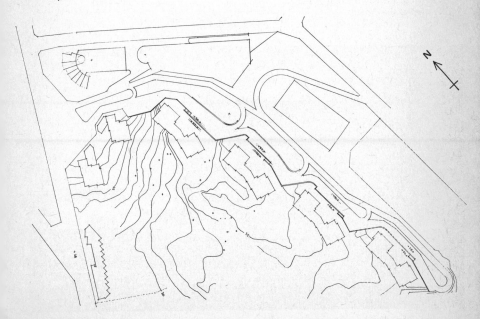

Björnholm Housing Development
Designed 1959

The site for this project was on the western outskirts of Helsinki, set in the beautiful island landscape typical of Finland's southern coast. The housing development was intended to be in close contact with the sea and with nature. By means of earth-fill, the tiny islands would be transformed to provide sites for buildings, with lagoons on all sides. By careful adaptation of mounds and lagoons the housing groups would be separated and protected from the main road traversing the site.

Three different housing types were proposed, together with a small centre for business and hotel premises. The housing included a six-storey high-rise apartment block, a further development of the architect's apartment building in the Berlin Hansaviertel (1957).

Model showing main road and housing types: (top left) high-rise housing on an artificial promontory; (bottom left) shopping centre and hotel; (centre right) rented flats; (top right) island with terraced houses

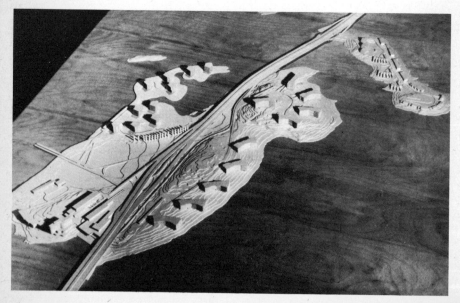

City Centre, Helsinki
Designed 1959—1964

The essential components of the designs for the new city centre were: the central square; Hesperia Park, with public buildings on the shores of Lake Töölö, which is preserved but reshaped; and the Kamppi district, the continuation of the old city centre. At the instigation of the city authorities the Pasila district was subsequently integrated in the overall plan, but with its own independent character.

The city's main thoroughfare is above the level of the railway lines, giving a panoramic view over the western and eastern parts of the city. The Kallio district is not visually separate from the other parts of the city, but forms — with the Töölö district — its inner core.

The public buildings are arranged in such a way that, when viewed from the main thoroughfare, they appear as the principal feature of the new city. There are two kinds of 'scenery' in the central area — the 'urban' and the 'original'. The former is the classical city centre, the latter a product of the 19th century, with the result that a tightly integrated urban layout was lacking. Hesperia Park and Lake Töölö were sentimentally preserved landscape features, and not part of a satisfying design.

Sketch layout

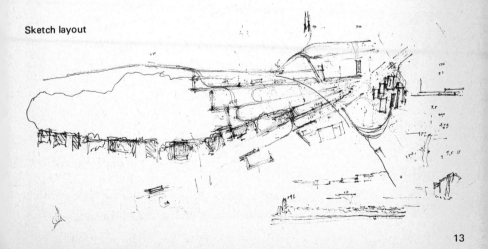

View of model, showing Lake Töölö and public buildings and business centre (in background), as seen from the main highway

Site plan

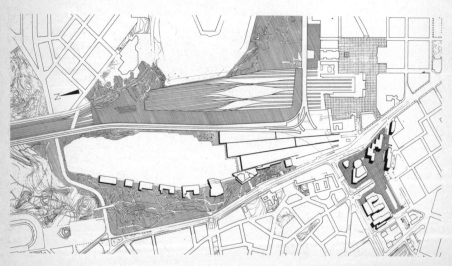

The public buildings on the edge of Hesperia Park project over the water, thus linking park and lake. An enlarged park will provide more space for pedestrians. Of the public buildings, the Concert Hall and the adjoining Convention Hall are located directly adjoining the triangular plaza and form its actual termination and principal accent. North of the Concert Hall there are planned, from south to north, an Opera House, Art Museum and Library, as well as a number of reserve buildings. Along the shore of the lake, beneath the public buildings, a pedestrian arcade has been created. The surface of the lake remains visible from the park through the arcades.

Detail of model seen from the north, with Hesperia Park in the foreground

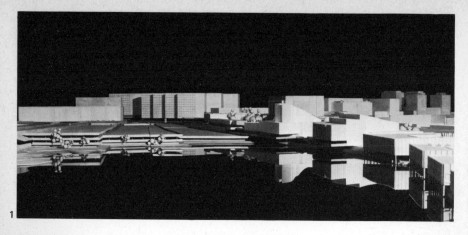

1 View of model, with the Kamppi district in the background
2 Detail of model
3 Plan at street level
4 View of model showing the bus terminal in the foreground

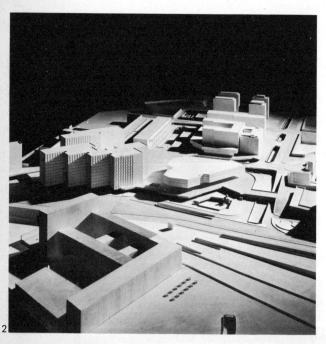

The Kamppi business district, already partly built, is the real focal point of the reorganized city centre. Pedestrians and traffic are kept separate, with the top deck reserved for pedestrians and a shopping precinct, and the lower deck for vehicles. Parking is provided at other levels.

Most of the Pasila area is taken up by the freight station. Other administrative facilities, e.g. transport organizations, not requiring a central location will also be located in Pasila; this district is being designed in detail by the municipal planning office.

4

1 Plan
2 Model showing the traffic arteries; in the background, the Kamppi district

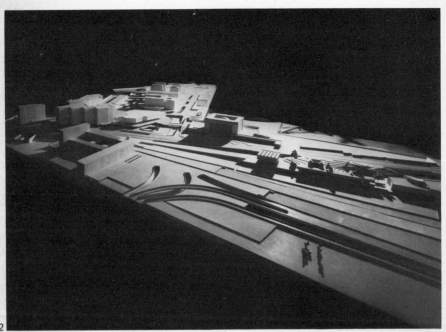

Cultural Centre, Leverkusen (Germany)
Competition 1962

The programme for the competition involved an exceptionally diverse and complex range of buildings, including a youth centre, an adult education centre, a large multi-purpose hall with a cinema, an experimental theatre, one large and one small theatre auditorium, with a large restaurant, a museum and the municipal library. The nature of the site has greatly limited the designs. The cultural centre, a place for contemplation and for human contact, ought to be situated in a quiet area, but this could not be achieved since the site is bounded on two sides by main traffic arteries and on the third by a railway. A quiet pedestrian zone, shielded as much as possible, was therefore provided along these three sides; as a shield against the railway an oversized 'foundation wall' was planned. Behind this wall was the intended site of the youth centre, the young people's school of music, the adult education centre and the multi-purpose hall. The museum and the municipal library were set along the Kölner Strasse and, next to them, would be the boundary zone with trees and shrubbery. Car parks would be provided under the terraced interior court.

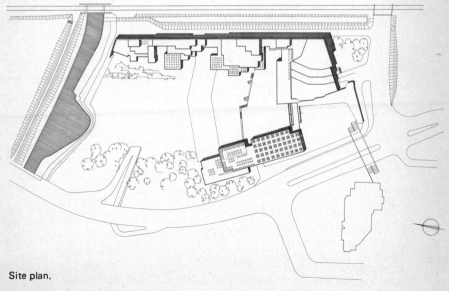

Site plan.

1 Main floor plan, with terraced court
2 Plan at street level
3 Elevation along the Kölner Strasse
4 Elevation along railway line, showing 'foundation wall'

1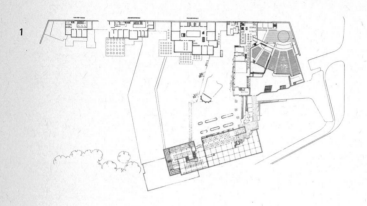

2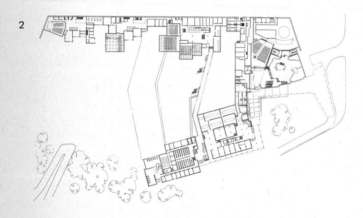

3

4

Town Centre, Rovaniemi
Designed 1963   Building begun 1965

The scheme is intended to form an administrative and cultural centre for Rovaniemi.
The town-hall tower and the theatre form extensions to the axis of the street, and
the two halves are separated by the fan-shaped library. The town-hall tower provides
the chief vertical accent in a scheme characterized by a general horizontal emphasis.

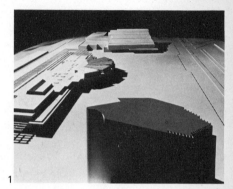

1 View of model from the town-hall tower
   towards the theatre
2 Site plan
3 View of model showing horizontal emphasis   1

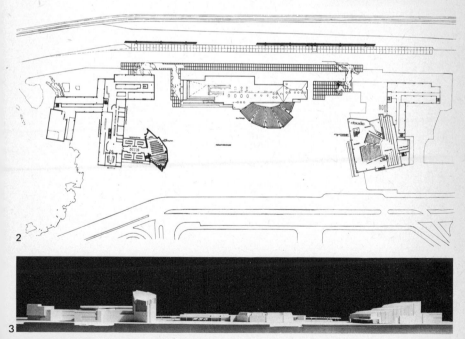

2

3

Administrative and Cultural Centre, Jyväskylä
Designed 1964   Under construction

As in many Finnish towns, the urban layout of Jyväskylä consists mainly of a series of squares. The new expanded administrative and cultural centre will form a square in the central part of the town.

The administration building is so designed that it can be extended at any time, being itself an extension of the existing town hall. The tower containing the council chamber is the dominating feature of the Town Hall Square; also situated on this square is the theatre, which can be adapted for many different purposes. The police headquarters will extend along the street and overlook the adjoining park. The Town Hall Square will become a central pedestrian area separating the two halves of the existing park.

General site layout

1 North elevation, with
   (right) the police
   headquarters, and (left)
   the municipal offices
2 Site plan at the level of
   the main square
   Scale 1:2,400
3 Cross-section through
   the council chamber
4 View of model, with the
   administration building
   (foreground) and tower
   containing the council
   chamber

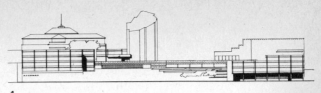

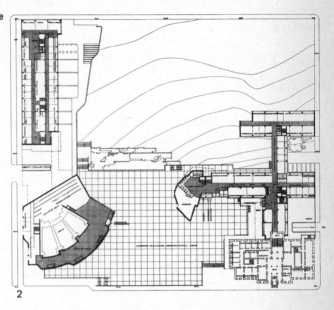

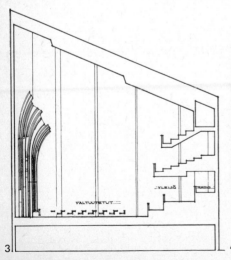

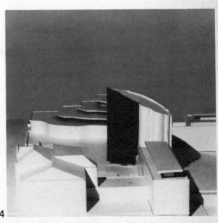

Town centre, Castrop-Rauxel (Germany)
Competition 1965

The interior organization envisages two separate pedestrian zones or squares and a peripherally sited car park area. The front of the administration building and the

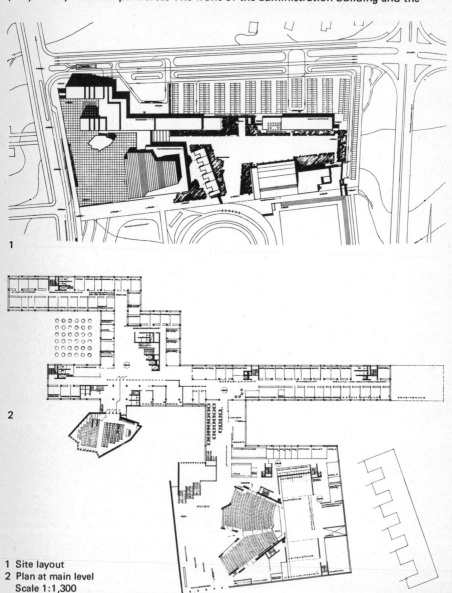

1 Site layout
2 Plan at main level
   Scale 1:1,300

town hall and the multi-purpose hall enclose the public square, which opens into the main roadway. The square is higher than the traffic level and has an entrance for special occasions. The second square, which opens into the sports centre with the stadium, has the character of a broad avenue. It is formed mainly by the sports arena and the public health centre. Moreover, a number of housing units have been proposed; these have deliberately not been included in the geometric organization.

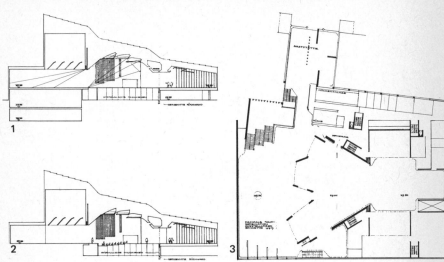

1 Section through hall, arranged as a banqueting hall
2 Section through hall, arranged for exhibitions with a small auditorium for lectures
3 Plan of the hall, showing how maximum flexibility can be achieved for multi-purpose use. The auditorium and stage have only a few supporting elements, and some floor sections can be raised or lowered as required
4 West elevation, seen from the main road, with the multi-purpose hall at the right
5 South elevation

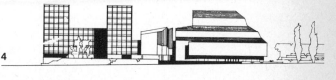

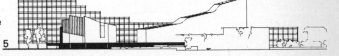

Housing development, Pavia (Italy)
Designed 1966

A satellite town for approximately 12,500 inhabitants is planned on the periphery of Pavia. The Milan-Rome highway runs straight through the centre of the envisaged 970,000 sq. metre site. On the south the area reaches the river Ticino. Owing to the

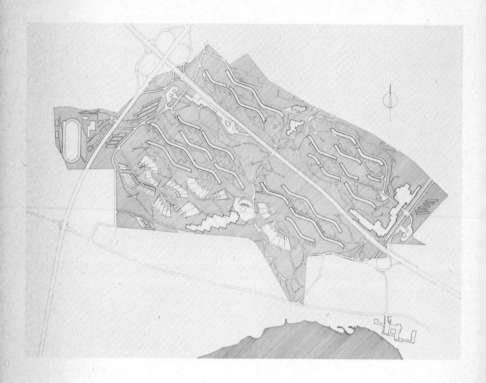

Site layout showing the housing arranged in a grid pattern parallel with the main highway, with pedestrian access at right angles to it. Access for vehicles is by parallel roads, but not between each block; there are two traffic arteries, one at the west and one at the east end of the site. Good separation is thus provided between pedestrians and vehicles.

height of the express highway, the houses have been designed following the same scheme as Baker House, the M.I.T. Senior Dormitory in Cambridge (Mass.). In order to eliminate the view on to this busy highway as much as possible, a curving shape was chosen. By this means no window would have an outlook directly on to the highway and traffic. The basic co-ordinating principle is a curving grid covering the entire site and derived ultimately from the form of the individual unit.

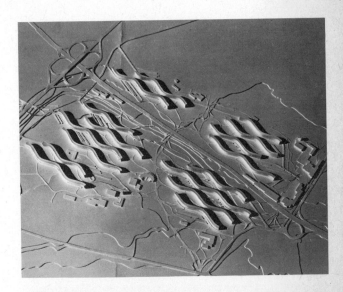

Model of first version, with standard curved buildings

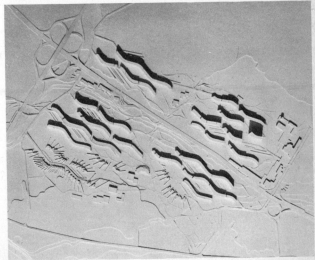

Model showing possible modification of the curves and alternative buildings, including single-family houses

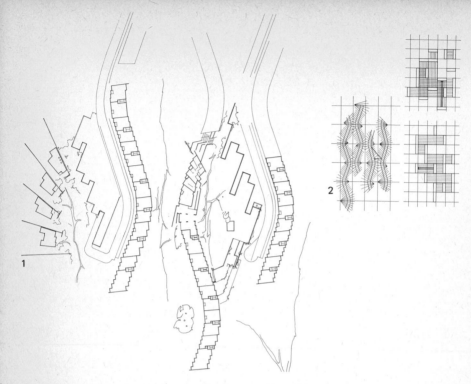

1

2

1 Detail plan of a housing group. The overlap of the curving grid pattern permits maximum expansion possibilities between housing blocks. Pedestrian pathways run through at ground-floor level. Scale 1:1,000
2 Comparative diagram showing the difference between the conventional rectangular grid with individual structures and a grid made up of continuous curves
3 Model viewed from the east
4 Model viewed from the west

3

4

Theatres and Cultural Buildings

Finnish Theatre, Turku
Competition 1927   Completed 1929

This theatre complex also includes a hotel, stores and offices, and forms part of a larger project. The theatre itself is intended for the private presentation of plays and play-readings, and the stage was therefore designed for recitation only. The auditorium consists of a simple cube with no decoration whatsoever; both wall and ceiling surfaces are in dark blue stucco. A system of golden lamps on golden standards forms the only decorative element in the room.
The spotlight system is housed in the ceiling in a sort of dome which takes a triangular form to correspond with the conically falling rays of the spotlights. The seating upholstery and the fabric wall covering of the stairways are in grey and pink.

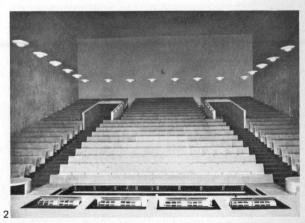

1 The stage lighting
2 The auditorium

Theatre and Concert Hall, Kuopio
Competition 1951 First prize Not built

Kuopio, a provincial city in central Finland, possesses a rich architectural heritage in its town hall dating from the mid-nineteenth century. It was planned to build a single-storey theatre and concert hall around the existing town hall in order to fill the architectural 'vacuum' behind it. With this arrangement a second Town Hall Square would have been created — as a counterpoint to the market place on the entrance side. The theatre and concert hall were placed on a corner of the steeply falling site in such a manner that an asymmetrical amphitheatre resulted, without ascending staircases, so that the entire internal circulation was contained on one level.

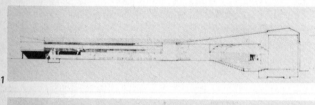

1

2

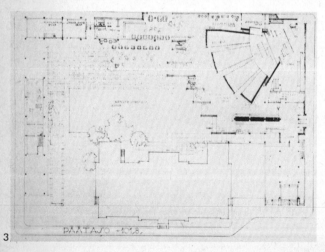

3

1 Section through
  theatre
2 Elevation of existing
  town hall
3 Plan at main level,
  with the theatre to
  the right

'House of Culture', Helsinki
Designed and built 1955—1958

This building, the 'Kultuuritalo', is a meeting place for several trade unions. The main objective was the creation of a large hall to be used both for concerts and congresses. These different uses require acoustics suitable both for music and the spoken word. From these considerations the interior took the form of a clam shell. Specially designed wall and ceiling surfaces serve for both absorption and reflection of the sound waves.

The architecturally rhythmical handling of the interior space has been designed in such a manner that the various types of wall surfaces can be interchanged to take care of the acoustics depending on whether the hall is full or empty. The asymmetrical amphitheatre receives its exterior form by close adherence to the form of the interior space. Because the building mass is such a monolith of varying curvatures, a special basic building block had to be developed. This basic building block is a brick designed to conform to every curve, whether concave or convex.

Auditorium and canopy over the main entrance

1

2

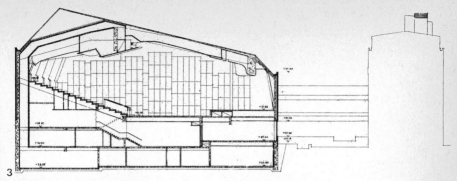

3

1 Detail of auditorium, showing junction of wall and timber ceiling
2 Interior view of the large auditorium. The front rows of seats are removable. On the wall are special acoustic elements
3 Section through the auditorium
4 Plan of the complex with the large auditorium and the office wing

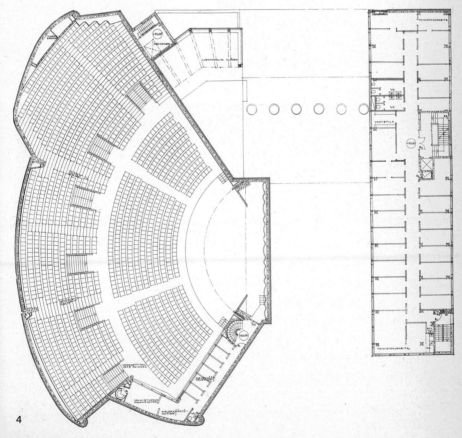

4

1 Detail of exterior, showing use of
  special bricks for the curved walls
  of the auditorium
2 General view of exterior of the
  auditorium

Cultural Centre, Wolfsburg (Germany)
Competition 1958   Built 1959–1962

The Wolfsburg Cultural Centre forms part of a planned larger complex, the final form of which has not as yet been determined.
The cultural centre has been built with the intention of providing a place for intellectual stimulus and for relaxation in the otherwise monotonous routine of working and living in an industrial city. Although an enclosed structure, it is intended that it should assume the role of an ancient Greek agora (an open, outdoor place).
The main building is divided in four sectors: (1) the municipal library as dominant element with a small school for adult education, (2) a group of hobby rooms, (3) a group of club and meeting rooms and (4) rooms and roof garden for community events. The various parts of the building are functionally related one to the other, and for this reason they all form part of the same building complex.

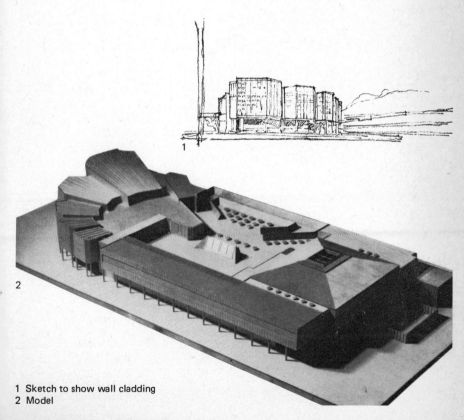

1 Sketch to show wall cladding
2 Model

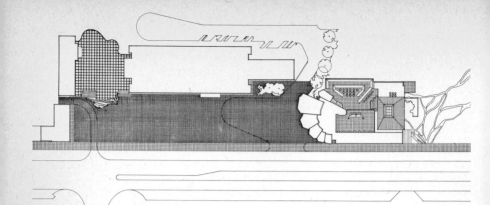

1

2

1 Site layout
2 View from the town hall into the upper level court
3 Elevation of the lecture halls on the Town Hall Square
4 View of the court, looking towards the youth centre
5 Longitudinal section. At ground level are the entrance foyer, the multi-purpose hall and the foyer of the youth centre. At upper-floor level are the main lecture hall, the court and the workshops of the youth centre
6 Upper floor, to the left the lecture rooms of the adult education centre, to the right the workshops and clubrooms. In the middle is the court for various types of activity

3

4

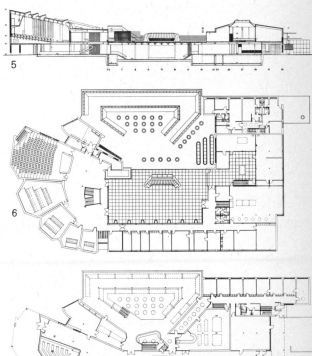

5

6

7　Plan at entrance level,
to the left the entran-
ces to the library and
lecture halls, to the
right the entrances to
the 'youth house',
children's library and
the caretakers' apart-
ments. Shops are
along the street,
under the arcade

1 Main entrance foyer with stairway to the lecture halls
2 Library
3 Vestibule of the workshop area in the youth centre. The skylight can be completely opened in summer
4 Detail of the large lecture hall, showing the film projection booth at the rear

Opera House, Essen (Germany)
Competition 1959   1st Prize   Designed 1961—1964

The Opera House will be sited in a large park. Vehicular and pedestrian traffic are completely separate, and the access to the main entrance is so planned that a great number of automobiles can be accommodated under the Opera's overhanging roof. The audience seating area is an asymmetrical amphitheatre with an undulating rear wall of loges and loge-like balconies. With this asymmetrical form, there is created a seating area which, even with a small audience, would not appear empty.
The audience seating area consists of two main elements: a dome-like room, kept in a deep-blue colour (indigo) and so designed as to easily accommodate both absorbent and reflective acoustic surfaces (dark, neutral colours). Contrasted with this dark background is the wall of loges in white marble, partly massive and partly broken up in a sort of filigree.

Sketch of site layout

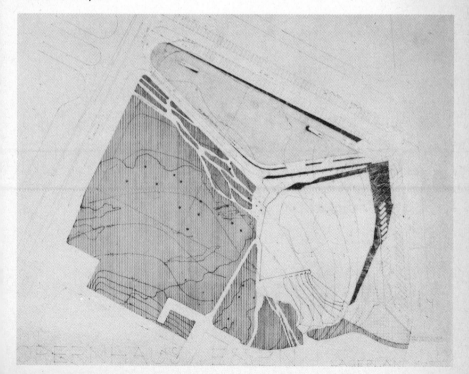

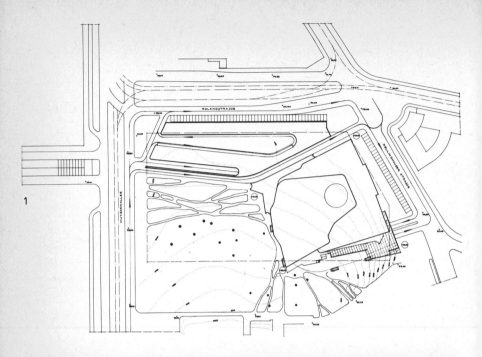

1

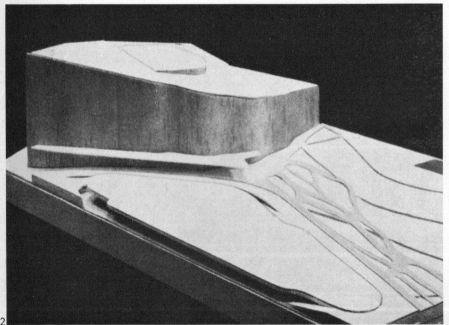

2

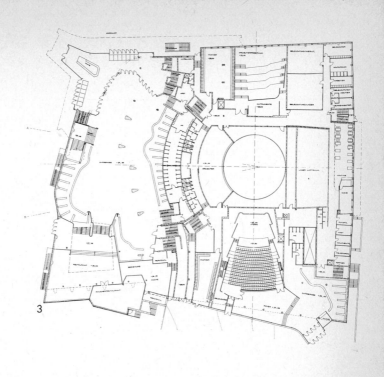

3

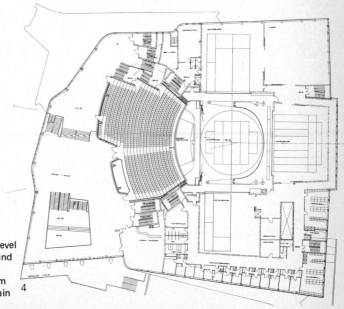

1 Site plan
2 Model
3 Plan at entrance level
  with cloakroom and
  studio stage
4 Plan at auditorium
  level, with the main
  foyer

4

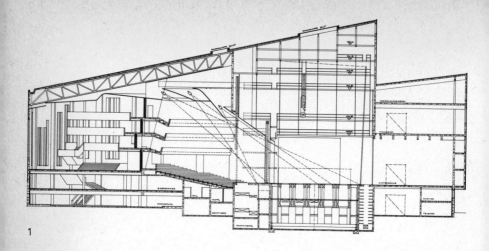

1

1 Section through Opera House
2 Drawing showing seating area and main foyer
3 Detail of model, showing proposed relief finish for walls of auditorium
4 Detail of model, showing main foyer and galleried construction

2

3

4

Scandinavia House, Reykjavik (Iceland)
Designed 1962/63   Built 1965–1968

Scandinavia House in Reykjavik is conceived as a small convention hall. The building was a gift from all the Scandinavian Governments to Iceland. It contains a lecture and display hall, a library with a Scandinavian collection, various clubrooms and a cafeteria.

1 Site plan
2 Entrance elevation

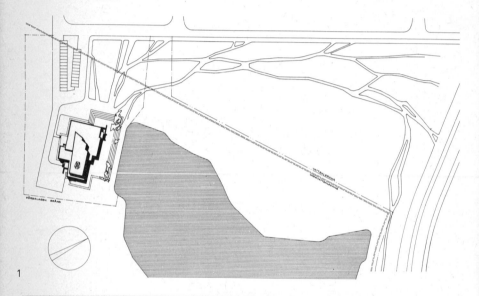

1

2

44

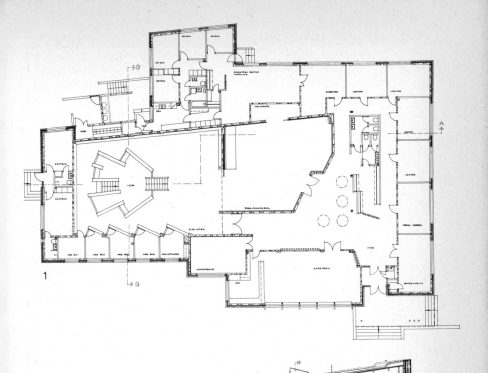

1 Plan
2 Longitudinal section
3 Entrance hall
4 Library

Concert and Convention Hall, Helsinki
Designed 1962   Built 1967–1971

The building forms part of the newly designed city centre; the trees on the site were preserved. A pedestrian zone runs longitudinally along Hesperia Park between Mannerheim Street and the Concert Hall. The main hall has an audience capacity of 1,750, and there is also a smaller auditorium, for recitals or chamber music, seating 350, and a subdivisible restaurant with space for up to 300 people.
The structure of the two auditoria is isolated from the rest of the building and given special acoustic joints down to foundation level in order to eliminate any possible disturbance from outside. The external facing is of white marble and black granite.

Site plan. Scale 1:4,000

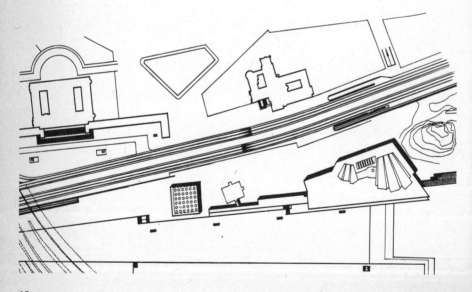

1
View from lake Töölö

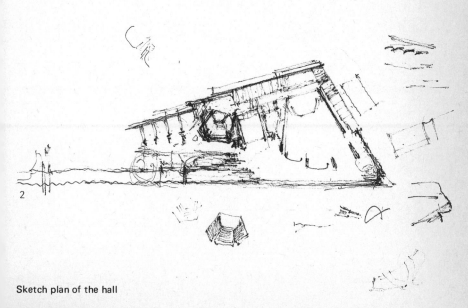

2

Sketch plan of the hall

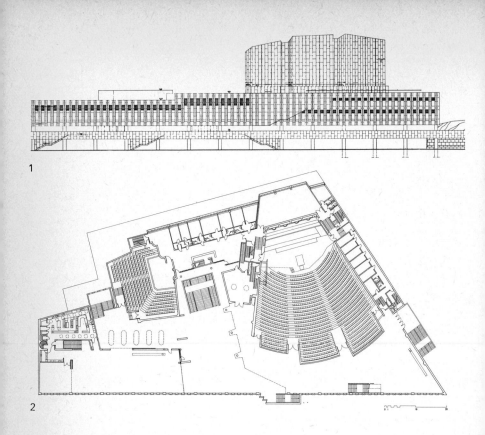

1

2

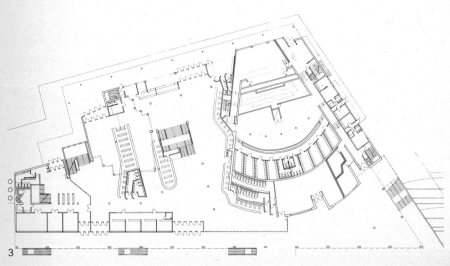

3

48

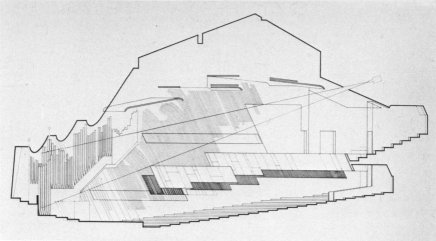

4

1 Drawing of façade
2 Plan of main floor
3 Plan at entrance level; each of the three main areas has a separate entrance, if required, on
the long side of the building
4 Section through the concert hall
5 Interior of large auditorium

5

1 Chamber-music room
2 View of façade

Cultural Centre, Siena (Italy)
Competition 1966

A most unusual site was chosen for the proposed new cultural centre: this was the vast enclosed court formed by the ramparts of a fortress built by Duke Cosimo I in 1560 outside the limits of the medieval city. This courtyard could easily accommodate the city's famous Piazza del Campo.

Preliminary sketch

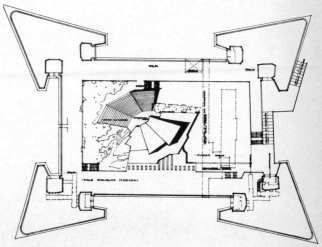

Site plan, showing the cultural centre within the existing ramparts.
Scale 1:2,800

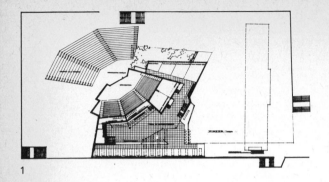

1

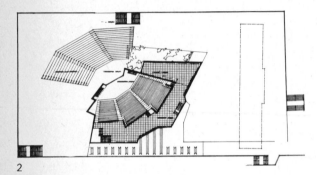

2

1 Plan at entrance level.
  The rear wall of the
  stage can be opened
  to form a single stage
  with that of the open-
  air theatre
2 Plan at foyer level.
  From the foyer there
  is a view of the
  medieval buildings
  of the old city
3 Cross-section. The
  courtyard would be
  partially filled in,
  level with the top
  of the ramparts
4 Elevation. The smooth
  white cube of the new
  building is intended
  to contrast with the
  weathered stone of
  the 16th-century
  fortress

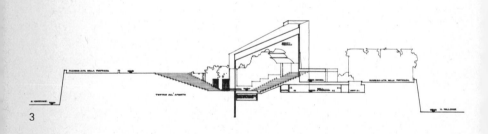

3

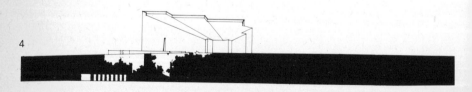

4

Theatre, Wolfsburg (Germany)
Competition 1966

The main problem involved in this assignment was to adapt the theatre building to the visual aspect of the city. The large intersection here cuts off the direct connection with the already built cultural centre and the Town Hall square. The theatre is located at a slight diagonal angle to the axis of the main thoroughfare. The open space leading towards the theatre causes the visual accent to fall on the prominent hill constituting the background and at the same time defining the limit of the city centre.
Pedestrian access to the theatre is partly above street level and partly below.

1 Rough sketch. Cross-section and elevation from the main road, looking towards the theatre, with the hill in the background
2 Site plan

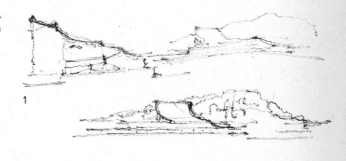

1

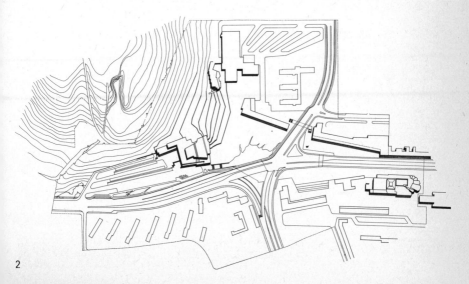

2

1 Plan at entrance level
2 Plan at main level
3 Elevation

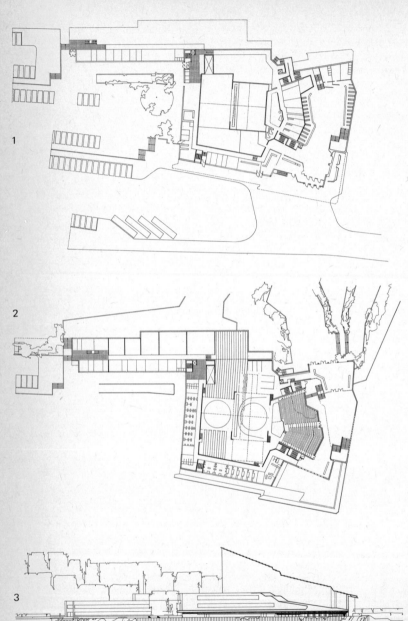

1

2

3

Theatre, Seinäjoki
Designed 1968/69

The theatre building, serving also as a convention hall and clubhouse, was planned to serve the city and its immediate environs. It is a small compact multi-purpose building, and in plan resembles the competition plan for the theatres in Wolfsburg and Essen. The interior appointments are simpler than in the above-mentioned buildings. This applies above all to the construction of the stage. It can be easily converted in various ways, and it is thus suitable for amateur theatrical productions.

1 Plan at auditorium level. The auditorium can be subdivided by means of a sliding wall
2 Plan at entrance level
3 Cross-section
4 Study model

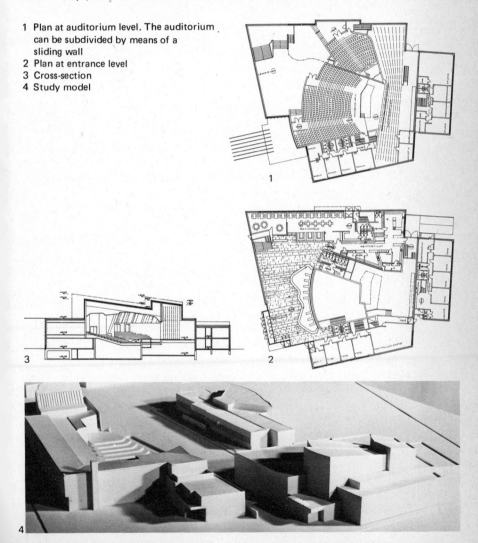

Exhibition Buildings and Museums

Exhibition '700 Years of Turku' 1929

The exhibition was set up in a park near the town centre and individual extensions stretched out into the immediate surroundings. In addition, visual symbols similar to the entrance structures were placed in central locations in the city so that the exhibition appeared to extend over a very large area.

The 700th Anniversary of the founding of Turku was also the occasion of a great music festival. For this event a large open-air-podium for choir and orchestra was erected. In order to achieve the greatest possible acoustical effects the form selected for this podium provided for two sounding boards: one curved surface served as a background while the other served as the podium itself.

1 The timber-built stage for choral and
   concert performances
2 General view

Finnish Pavilion at the Paris World's Fair 1937
Competition 1935   1st Prize   Built 1936/37

The Exhibit took place partly in closed-in buildings and partly under the open sky in such a way that the visitor hardly noticed the change from interior room to open space. Architecturally, it was not the main composition which dominated — it was rather the individual groupings and the series of posts which were so conceived as to emphasize Finnish timber as both a structural element and wall surfacing.
In an Exhibition the movement of the stream of visitors is not merely a traffic problem; unobstructed viewing of objects on display must also be considered.

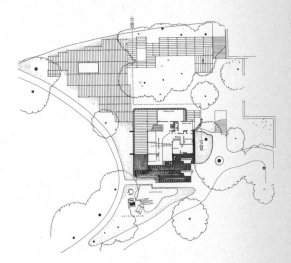

Plan at upper-floor level

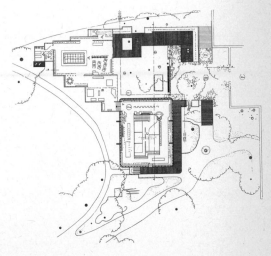

Plan at ground level

4

1 Column connectors
2 Columns and supporting elements
3 Diagonal struts
4 Wall cladding of the main building
5 Interior court and book exhibit

5

Finnish Pavilion at the New York World's Fair 1939
Competition 1937   Built 1938/39

The Pavilion, 52 ft high, consisted of four storeys in all. The uppermost series of
photographs showed the Country; the next, the People; the third, somewhat lower
down, Work, and finally the bottom series depicted the results of the above three
factors — the Products. By the use of free architectural forms and sloping wall
surfaces the uppermost series of photographs and products were as easily seen by the
spectator as were those on the lower walls. The pictorial presentations and the
various products displayed had simultaneously both a vertical and horizontal
relationship.
An exhibition should be what in the early days it used to be: a general store, in which
all possible objects are grouped together in a dense display — whether it be fish,
cloth or cheese. Therefore in this pavilion I have attempted to provide the
densest possible concentration of display, a space filled with wares, next to and
above and beneath each other, agricultural and industrial products often just a
few inches apart. It was no easy work — composing the individual elements into
one symphony.

1 Plan at entrance level
      1/3/7 Information desks
         2 Office
  4/8/9/10 Exposition platforms
         5 Toilets
         6 Kitchen
2 View from the entrance towards the undulating wall
3 Plan of the balcony restaurant
     7/16 Information desks
       11 Projector cabin
   12/13 Restaurant
       14 Counter
       15 Exposition gallery
       17 Exposition hall

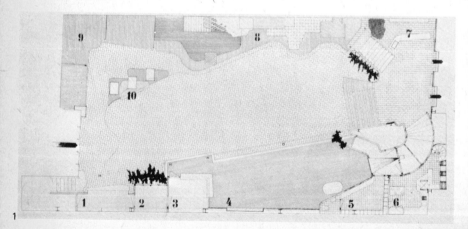

1

2

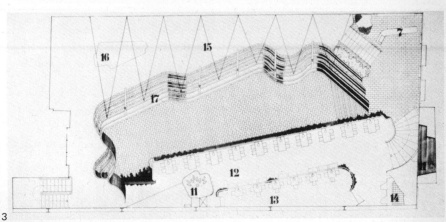

3

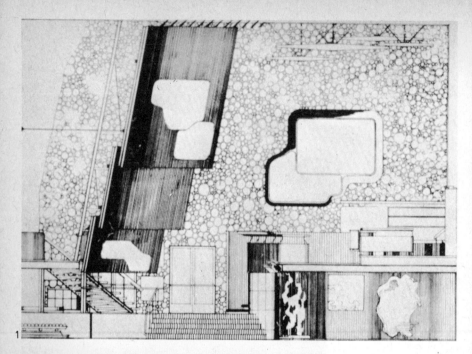

1 Section
2 View from the exit
towards the informa-
tion desk, the restau-
rant gallery and film
cabins
3 View of the exit and
the undulating wall

62

3

1/2 Exhibits displayed below
the undulating wall

64

Art Gallery, Reval (Tallinn), Estonia
Competition 1936

The special layout of the gallery affords the visitor free choice as to which section he would like to see. The entrance hall is architecturally so formed that the visitor, immediately upon entry, gains a perspective view of the entrances to the various exhibits as well as of the individual sections. Also, all rooms of the museum are connected by means of a continuous visitors' path.

1 Model
2 Perspective of entrance hall. The entrances to the various departments of the museum can be seen

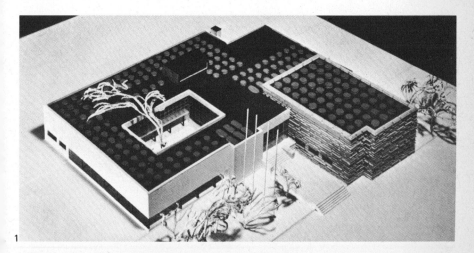

1

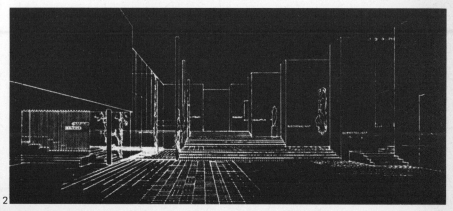

2

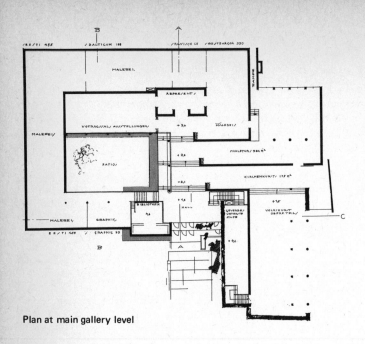

Plan at main gallery level

Plan at access level

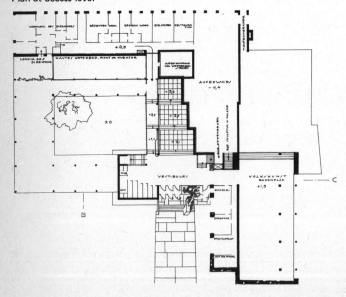

Museum, Aalborg (Denmark)
Competition 1958   Built 1969–1973

Light has the same significance for an art museum as acoustics for a concert hall.
It changes its character depending on the direction from which it comes. Because
of this an asymmetrical lighting system was devised for this museum.
The north-east light, entering from above, illuminates the halls with diffused light
during the daily hours of opening. Sunlight from the south and west is utilized
indirectly by means of reflecting ceiling and wall surfaces. The lighting for the
main exhibition hall was determined essentially by the building's location and
surroundings; the high, beech-forested slopes form a natural wall and the many
colours changing with the seasons lend an unusual liveliness to the light in this
valley. Because the main exhibition hall receives a good overall light from all
directions (except from the south), all walls can be used for display.

Overall view

1 Design sketch
2 Partial view with, right, the summer open-air theatre
3 View from north-east
4 Interior view of an exhibition room
5 Entrance hall with the 'Three women' by Lynn Chadwick

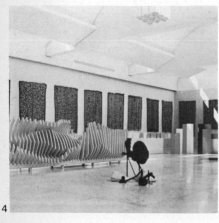

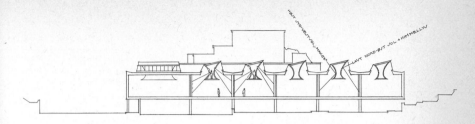

Section through the
exhibition hall

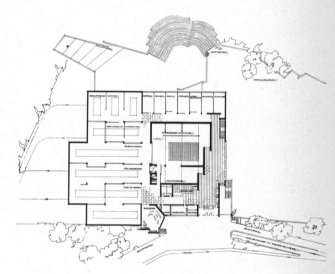

Plan at main level

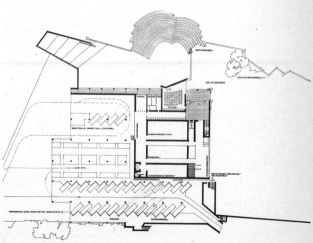

Plan at lower level

Central Finnish Museum, Jyväskylä
Designed 1959   Built 1960–1962

The Central Finnish Museum is a small museum built with a modest budget. It is
designed to accommodate special travelling exhibitions, and contains a Central
Finnish folklore collection. The museum stands on a wooded slope. Special care
was taken to spare the trees when the building was planned. The walls are mainly
rendered both outside and inside. All rendered surfaces, framed concrete parts and
timber cladding are painted white.

1 Plan at main level
2 Plan at basement level
3 Exterior view

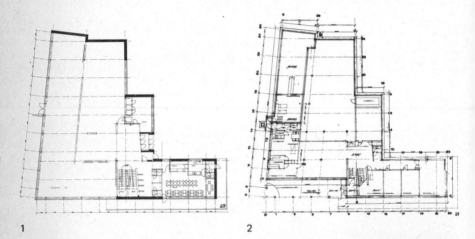

1   2

3

1 Exterior view
2 The lower part of the exhibition hall
3 The large exhibition hall

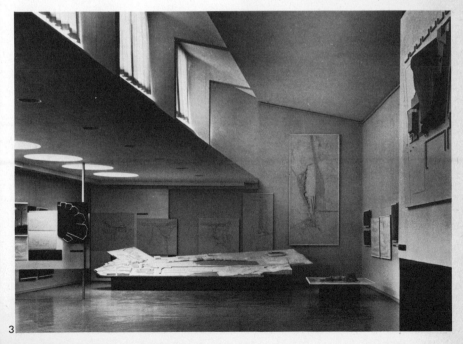

Art Gallery, Shiraz (Iran)
Designed 1970

The hill-top site for the art gallery is outside the city, near the new university. The hillside is to be artificially irrigated and developed as a public park.
The design of the gallery permits internal subdivision to create individual display areas, and from the main entrance the visitor will have a clear view through the entire building. Since the plan of the gallery does not impose any viewing sequence, the interior can be adapted for any kind of exhibition.

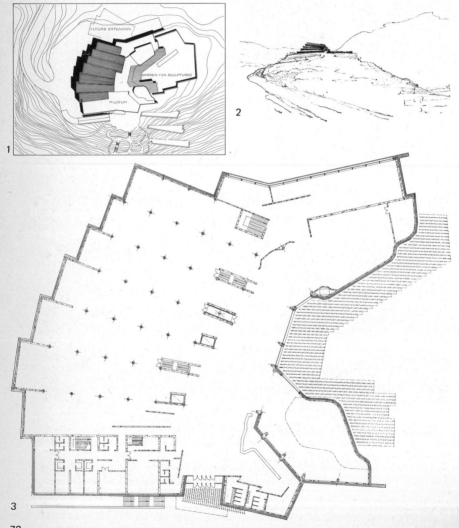

1

2

3

1 Site plan
2 Preliminary sketch made on the site
3 Plan of main floor, showing subdivisible display area, administrative offices, lecture hall and special exhibition hall. Scale 1:900
4 Section. The roof of the display area is glazed, with a system of slats and reflectors to counteract direct sunlight; artificial lighting is also installed at ceiling level
5 Elevation seen from the sculpture garden
6 Elevation of entrance front
7 Model

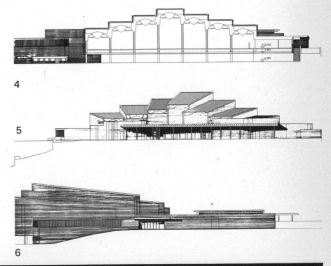

4

5

6

7

Sanatorium

Tuberculosis Sanatorium, Paimio
Competition 1928   Built 1929—1933

The basic architectural idea consisted primarily of a harmonious combination of service and quiet zones. The main element in the building conception is the individual patient's room. Although three-bed rooms provide more flexibility in accommodating patients, two-bed rooms were selected because they offer more quiet.
An extended period of confinement can be extremely depressing for a bed-ridden patient. Furthermore, conventional hospital rooms are never designed for constantly bed-ridden patients. The contrasts in colour and mass between vertical walls

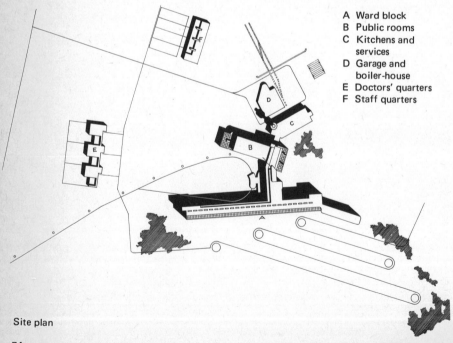

A Ward block
B Public rooms
C Kitchens and
   services
D Garage and
   boiler-house
E Doctors' quarters
F Staff quarters

Site plan

and horizontal ceilings resulting from both natural and artificial light are not particularly well-suited for patients who are especially sensitive because of the nature of their illness.

The rooms and apartments of the personnel are located so as to be least affected by the sanatorium atmosphere. The senior personnel, including the doctors, are located in row houses having no view of the sanatorium.

1 Typical plan of
  upper floors
2 Ground-floor plan
3 Section through the
  ward block

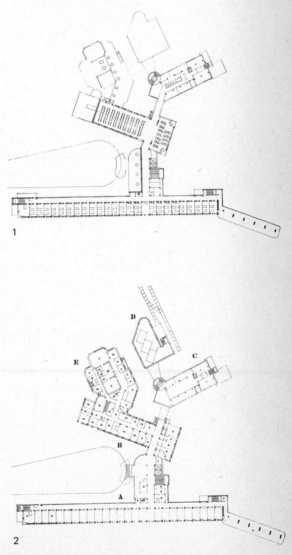

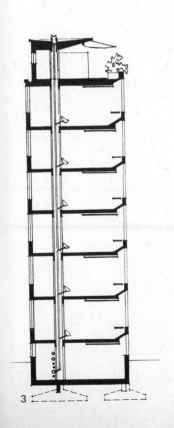

1 East elevation
2 View from the west

1 The main staircase
2 Open terrace on the
   south side of the
   wards

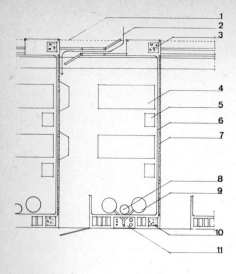

Plan of typical ward:
1 Venetian blinds
2 Fresh-air-intake
3 Structural column
4 Bed
5 Bedside table
6 Soft surface to wall
7 Hard surface to wall
8/9 Wash basins
10 Structural column
11 Plumbing duct

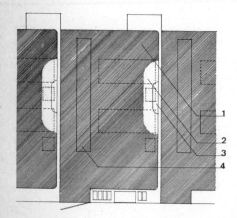

1 Ceiling painted dark
2 Bright, reflecting zone of ceiling
3 Light fitting
4 Ceiling radiant-heating panel

Typical ward

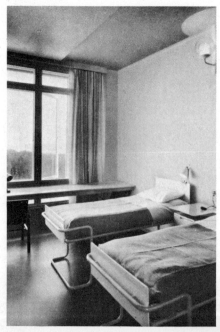

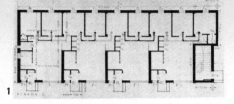

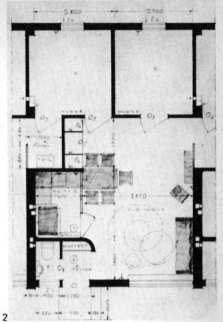

1 Plan of terraced staff quarters
2 Plan of a typical staff house
3 Terrace of houses

Educational Facilities

College of Education, Jyväskylä
Competition 1950   Built 1953–1956

The Institute is laid out in the form of a 'U', built around a campus. It incorporates a main building with the most important teaching departments, library and experimental school, sports facilities with enclosed swimming pool, dormitories as well as clubs. In order to underline the significance of the Institute in the urban setting, the main entrance has been treated as an extension of the main street of the town. The various buildings each have two entrances, one out to the parking areas and streets and another to the interior court reserved for pedestrians.

Site plan: (left) dormitories and refectory; (above left) gymnasium and swimming pool; (bottom right) classrooms, library and auditorium; (top right) associated school buildings

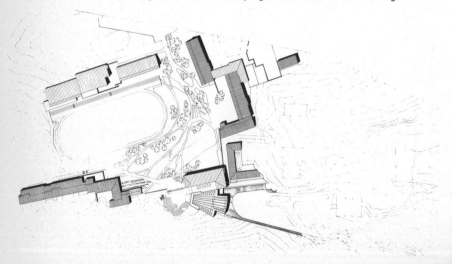

1 Plan of classrooms
2 View from the covered way, looking towards the sports centre
3 View from the playing field, looking towards the staff dining hall (left) and the students' dining hall

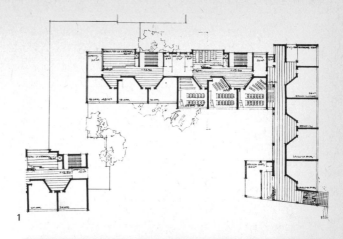

1

2

3

1 Foyer between the
  auditorium and the
  classroom block
2 Entrance hall and
  foyer

Institute of Technology, Otaniemi
Designed 1955   Built 1961—1964

The square on one side of the main building is reserved for motor vehicles; on the opposite side is the pedestrian zone, which is terraced and laid out like a park. It connects the main building with the facing residential complex.
The principal element of the entire complex is the auditorium group. The two auditoria are disposed in an arc and stepped in the manner of an amphitheatre. The roof structure is also stepped in a similar manner, and the entire roof forms a backdrop to the students' meeting place behind. The administration building also faces this area, thus forming an inner court.
The actual classroom premises are grouped about smaller intermediate courts. Within these groups are also situated the secondary lecture halls and laboratories. The buildings are divided into four main sections: administration; general studies; geography department; and architecture department. The buildings of each department are so arranged that future expansion is possible for any one without affecting the others.

Site plan

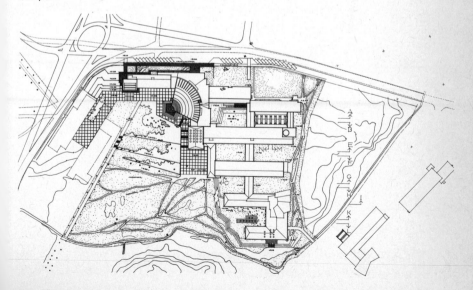

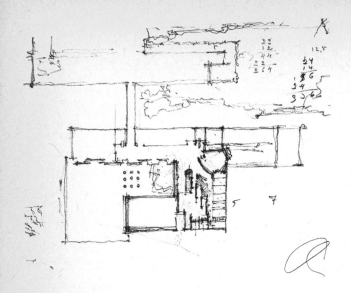

Design sketch of the entrance to the
architecture department

Exterior, showing the main auditorium

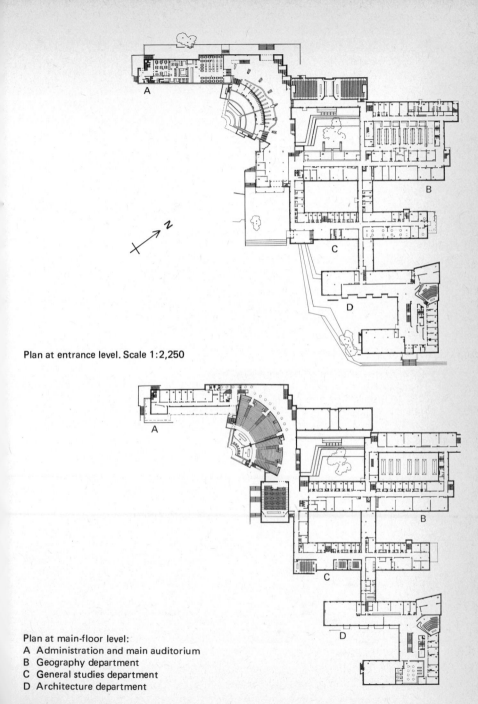

Plan at entrance level. Scale 1:2,250

Plan at main-floor level:
A Administration and main auditorium
B Geography department
C General studies department
D Architecture department

1 Rear of the main
   auditorium
2 Main auditorium
3 Foyer of the main
   auditorium
4 Lecture theatre
   with skylights. The
   ventilation system
   is installed in the
   suspended ceiling

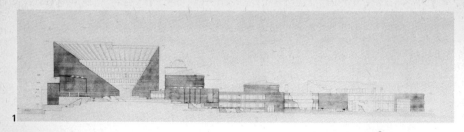

1 South elevation, showing (left) the main auditorium, (centre) the geography department, and (right) the architecture department

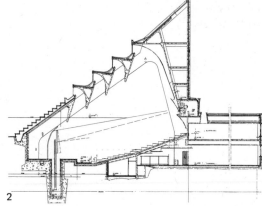

2 Cross-section through the main auditorium. The lower part of the roof is stepped to form an open-air theatre
3 Interior of the main auditorium

Students' Union of Västmanland-Dala, Uppsala (Sweden)
Designed 1961   Built 1963–1965

Two basic conditions had to be met in the choice of site and precise positioning of the building. The site was in the grounds of an old manor house which was demolished to make way for the new Union, the manor house having been its headquarters before the new building was erected. The garden had for long been a meeting place for the students, and the new Union was designed to blend with the existing layout.

1 Perspective sketch
2 Street façade

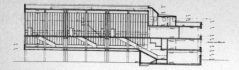

Longitudinal section

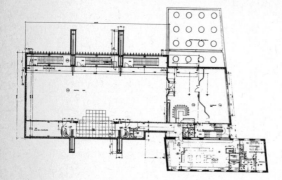

Plan at hall level

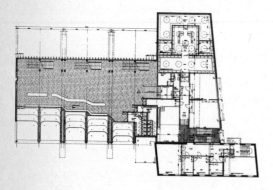

Plan at foyer level

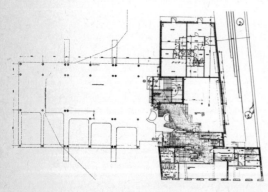

Plan at garden level with
the main entrances

1 Exterior view
2 Exterior elevation view
3 Street front with projecting boxes
  containing flexible partition units

1 Main hall
2 Foyer
3 Detail of glazed internal wall

92

Baker House, Massachusetts Institute of Technology, Cambridge (Mass.)
Built 1947/48

The site of this students' residence overlooks a busy road along the Charles River, and in order to avoid as far as possible windows with a direct view of the road, a curving plan was chosen. This decision was based on the principle that a diagonal line of sight is less trying to the eye when viewing moving objects.
Staircases are located on the north side of the building, providing an unobstructed view along the entire length of the building from the lowest landing.

1 Plan
2 The students' restaurant
3 Detail of rear façade

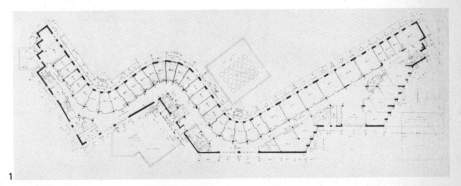

Hotel for Students, Otaniemi
Designed 1962   Built 1964—1966

This hotel for students was planned to supplement existing students' residences. It
is intended to serve as a guest house; moreover, individual guests as well as groups
can be accommodated here as in an ordinary hotel. The main entrance with the
reception desk and a small cafeteria are situated in a protected courtyard at
ground-floor level.
Each group has assigned to it a small kitchen and a common lounge. Each group can
be reached via a separate vertical access, without impinging on the other groups.

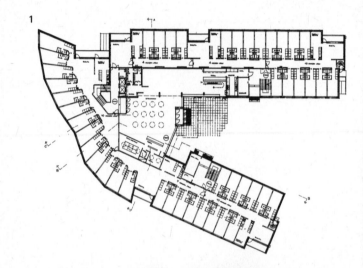

1 Plan at ground-
   floor level
2 Site plan
3 Elevation

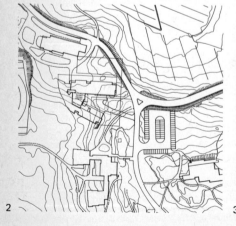

94

Institute of International Education, New York (USA)
Designed 1963   Built 1964/65

The Institute of International Education is located on the twelfth floor of the
United Nations Organization building. The work on the interior was financed by the
Edgar J. Kaufmann Foundation; the Foundation and the Institute's committee
requested that all interior fittings should be manufactured in Finland so as to give
a unity of style to the main hall and the various rooms. In addition, sculpturally
designed wall finishes and other fixtures were requested in order to enhance the
general appearance of the decor.

1 Drawing showing walls with decorative timber finish
2 Plan
3 Detail of the main hall

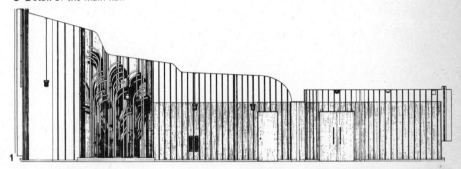

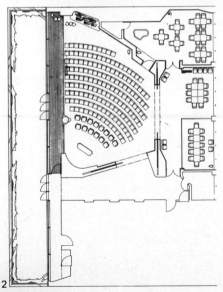

1 Detail of the
   decorative finish
2 Main hall

96

Libraries

Library, Viipuri (now Viborg, USSR)
Competition 1927   1st prize   Built 1930–1935

The building, which was destroyed during the Russo-Finnish War (1940–41), comprised a reading room and lending library on different levels together with a lecture hall, children's library, periodical room and administrative offices. The building was faced with white stucco, with the exception of the entrance area which was finished in natural stone.

1 Aerial view; on the right the cathedral
2 Main entrance; to the right the lecture hall

In order to understand the design fully, it is necessary to study the floor plans side by side. On the ground floor the main entrance formed the central axis, with the lending library and reading room above, the children's library had a separate entrance and the stockroom was located below the main entrance level.

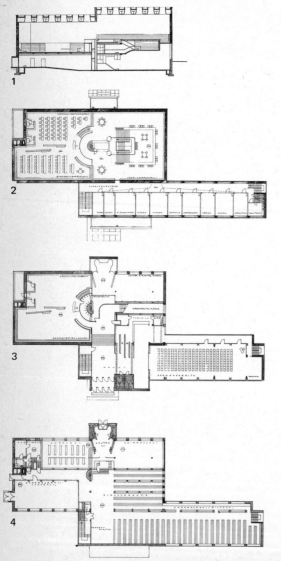

1 Longitudinal section through reading room and main library
2 Floor plan of the main library and reading room and administrative offices
3 Plan at entrance level, with lecture hall, reading room and children's library
4 Plan at lower-floor level, with stockroom and entrance to the children's library

The reading room was lit from above, natural daylight being diffused by conical, funnel-like skylights to provide shadow-free conditions at any point in the room; these skylights also provided shadowless illumination of the book-stacks, even when a person was standing directly in front of the shelves. The artificial lighting system was designed to provide similar shadow-free reading conditions.

1 The skylights on the roof
2/3 Sketches showing illumination with natural and artificial lighting

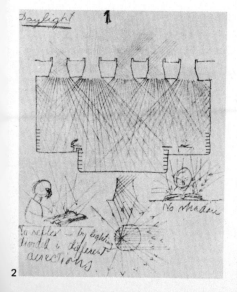

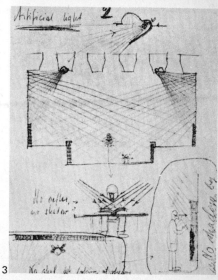

The lecture hall served not only for speeches and lectures, but was also very often used for discussion evenings. The undulating ceiling of thin wooden strips was so designed that every point in the room was acoustically 'alive'.

1 The lecture hall
2 Acoustic diagram
3 Detail of the undulating ceiling of the lecture hall

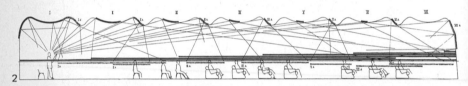

1 Main reading room
2 Stairs in the main library leading to
  the reading room
3 Glazed stair tower

Library, Seinäjoki
Designed 1963   Built 1963–1965

The library is a part of the administrative and cultural centre. The blankwall façade of the library constitutes the south side of the town hall square. The offices and the smaller halls are accommodated in a rectangular block. On the south side is located the fan-shaped library hall.

1 Plan at main level. Scale 1:500
2 View of the administrative and cultural centre

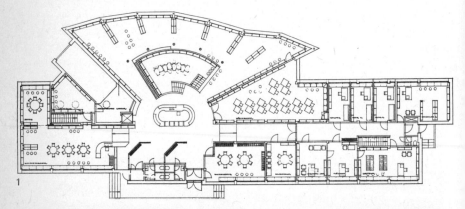

1 Detail section through the library
  and the reading area
2 Entrance elevation
3 Library elevation

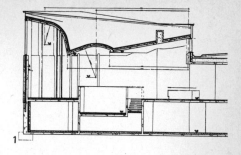

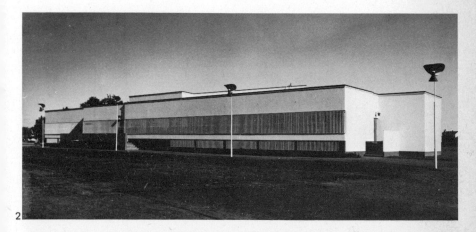

1 Interior of library
2 View from the sunken
  reading area

Library, Rovaniemi
Designed 1963   Built 1965–1968

The library in Rovaniemi is the first building of the planned administrative and cultural centre.
The main area, which looks on to the quiet central square, receives its light from the north. This section accommodates the libraries for children, young people and adult readers, along with the Lapland Collection and the reading room. On the main level there are also work rooms and studies, conference and small reading rooms, the administration with a cafeteria, the travelling library, a small kindergarten, a lecture and display room and the Arctic Bird Collection. The music library and the Geological Museum are at basement level.
The museum areas are so designed that they can be converted at any time into library premises.

1 Plan at main level. Scale 1:800
2 The entrance front

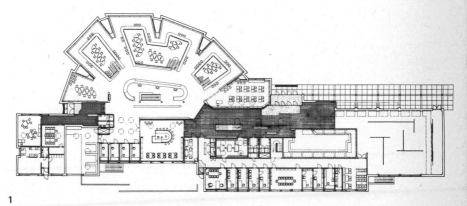

1

2

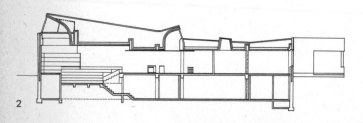

1 Sketch plan
2 Cross-section
3/4 Entrance lobby

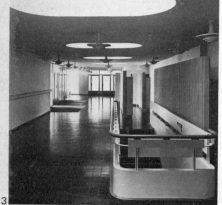

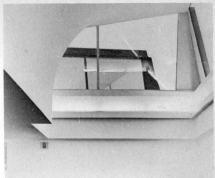

1/2 Views of the main library
3   View of the circulation department in
    the main library

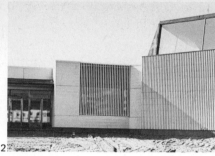

1   Access to main entrance
2/3 Details of exterior, showing
     library skylights

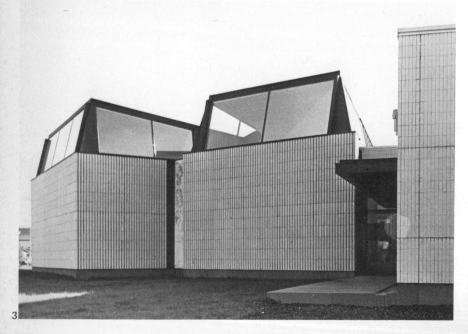

Library of the Institute of Technology, Otaniemi
Designed 1964   Built 1965—1969

The library building, which is closely related to the other main buildings of the
Institute (see p. 83), is situated parallel to an old avenue which had formerly led to
the centre of a large estate, and it forms one side of a large park.
There are two entrances, one from the pedestrian area on the park side, the other
from the access road and car park. All large windows and skylights face the park.
Internally, the library stacks are arranged on an open-access basis for all students, with
a lending department and the administrative offices at first-floor level; there are also
lecture rooms, research rooms, record-listening cubicles etc. at ground-floor level.
The construction of the library completed the complex of new buildings for the
Institute of Technology.

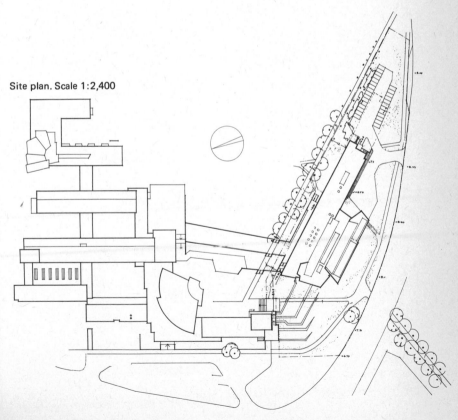

Site plan. Scale 1:2,400

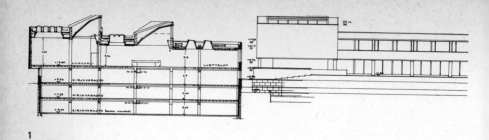

1

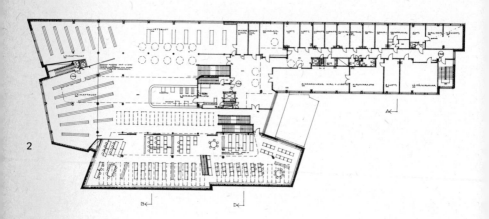

2

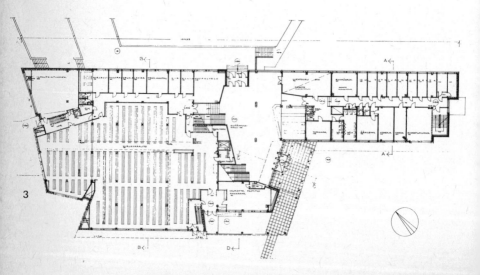

3

110

1 Cross-section
2 Plan at first-floor level. Scale 1:850
3 Plan at entrance level
4 Entrance hall
5 Main reading room
6 Circulation desk with view into the large reading room

1 Pedestrian access on the park side, and the old avenue
2 Main entrance seen from the road

Library of Mount Angel Benedictine College, Mount Angel, Oregon (USA)
Designed 1965/66   Built 1967—1970

The library of Mount Angel Benedictine College, which was founded in the last century, is situated in the centre of the campus. From the front, only the one-storey annexes are visible; the actual library is accommodated on the steep slope Owing to this disposition of the new building, it does not conflict with the original buildings on the site.

1 View of the library built into the steeply sloping site
2 Model

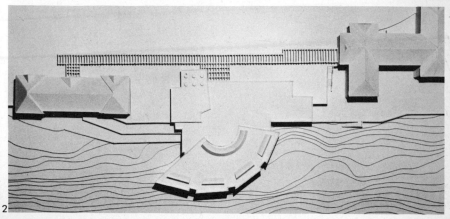

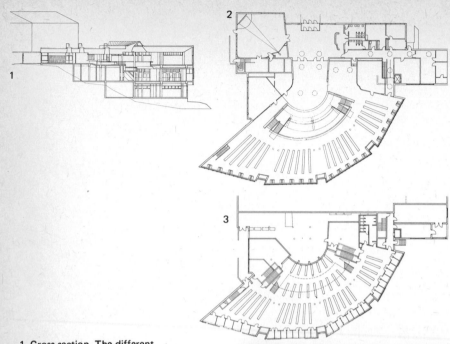

1 Cross-section. The different
  levels in the library conform
  to the contours of the site
2 Plan at entrance level, with
  the administrative offices, a
  lecture hall and the library.
  Scale 1: 1,000
3 Plan at first basement level:
  the main library
4/5 Views of the central area
  with the reading gallery

Sports Centres

Gymnasium, Otaniemi
Commissioned 1949   Built 1950–1952

The gymnasium is the main building of the sports centre of Helsinki's Technical
High School. It was built for the Olympic Games in 1952 and serves all athletic
pursuits. The building derives its shape from the indoor track and the area
required for throwing the javelin. The construction: nailed timber trusses assembled
on the site and lifted into position.
The stands are arranged in a kind of mound linking the stadium with the indoor
tennis hall. This enables spectators to follow events in both halls without excessive
circulation.

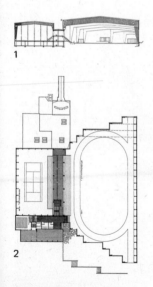

1 Cross-section of stadium
2 Plan of stadium
3 Model of gymnasium
4 Interior

Vogelweidplatz Sports and Concert Centre, Vienna (Austria)
Competition 1953   1st prize   Not built

A large, covered sports hall was called for which could also serve as a concert hall
with 25.000 seats and, together with the many auxiliary rooms, could also be used
as an exhibition building. In addition, there were to be spaces devoted to conventions,
aquatic sports and various other functions.
The project took the form of a combination amphitheatre-arena under a suspended
roof structure for concerts, the interior could be arranged for either complete or
partial seating. The roof structure, conceived in the manner of a suspension bridge,
covers a conglomeration of large and small halls.
The acoustics of the amphitheatre could be adapted to suit the needs of the occasion
by means of louvres suspended from the ceiling.
It was intended that access for vehicles would be underground, with stairways
leading up to the entrance piazza. This rectangular area was to be at road level, with
pedestrian access from the street through a garden for those arriving by public
transport.
The particular features of this design were the suspended copper roof and the
sloping walls of the auditorium.

Model seen from the south-east. In the foreground is the access ramp for cars, and above it the
swimming pool on one side of the entrance piazza; behind the main amphitheatre are open-air
tennis courts

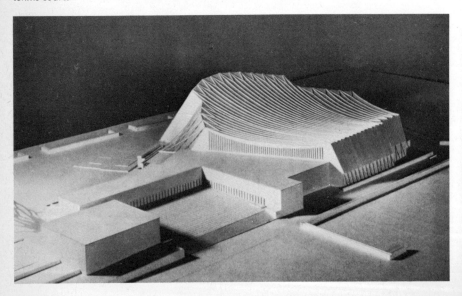

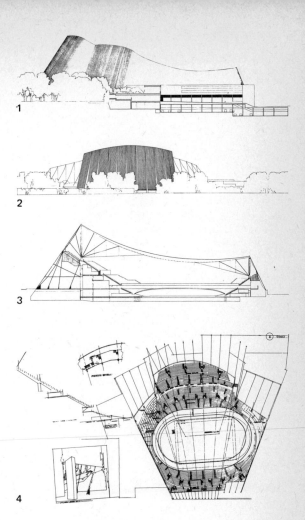

1 South elevation of the main hall.
  The covered car park is situated
  below the entrance piazza; also
  provided were box offices, administration, press and radio facilities,
  and (left) the restaurant
2 West elevation
3 Section through main hall
4 Plan of main hall
5 Plan at ground level. The swimming pool and bowling alley
  are at the left, with facilities
  for physical training, boxing,
  tennis etc. adjoining the main
  hall on the right

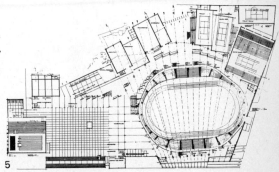

Office and Administration Buildings

Offices for the 'Turun Sanomat', Turku
Designed 1927/28   Built 1928/29

The office building for a Turku newspaper was the first by Aalto to attract attention from abroad.
The structural frame is of reinforced concrete and the outer insulating wall is of light-weight concrete. The surface of this porous material was covered with wire

1 Street front
2 Plan at entrance level, showing arrangement of structural columns
3 Main entrance from the street

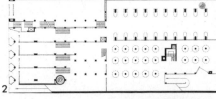

netting and covered with a special stucco containing a colour-tinted varnish. Various types of skylights are installed in the flat roofs. This was the first time Aalto had experimented with large, round skylights on a conical concrete base. In connection with flat slab construction, the reinforced concrete frame can exhibit either a symmetrical or asymmetrical column arrangement.

1 Experimental skylights, seen from outside
2 Skylights seen from inside
3 Storage space
4 Machine room
5 Detail of staircase

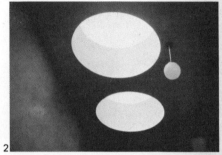

Finnish National Pensions Institute, Helsinki
Competition 1948   Built 1952–1956

The principal architectural problem was the creation of a large office complex for 800 employees in a crowded business area of the city. The entire building consists of several distinct parts and building masses, all grouped around a raised inner garden court, and contains a total of 3,880,000 cu. ft of office space. Internal circulation is provided between the different parts, some of it being below ground level. In the construction of this building a number of experimental features were adopted, e.g. the use of sound-absorbent walls to help create quiet working conditions, radiant heating with visible architectural forms, etc.

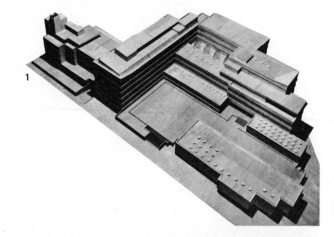

1 Model, showing the
  garden court
2 Entrance front

1 Cross-section through
main building
2 Plan of directors' floor
with conference rooms
3 Plan of typical office
floor

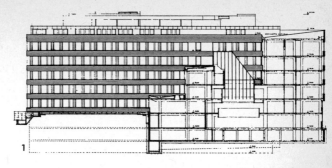

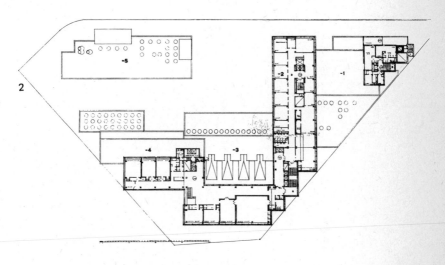

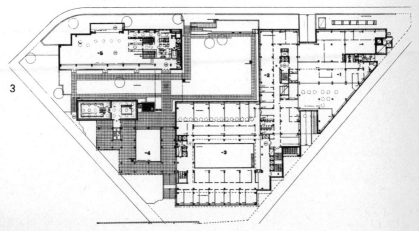

121

1 Stairs to restaurant
2 Sections through the skylight in the main hall
3 Staff restaurant
4 Main hall with interviewing cubicles
5 Reference library

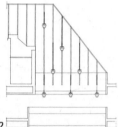

4

5

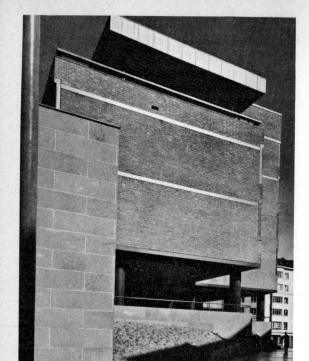

1 End elevation
2 Garden front

124

Rautatalo Building, Helsinki
Competition 1951   Built 1953—1955

One of the main problems was to design a commercial building combining shops and office space (the six upper floors) in a style which would blend with nearby office buildings in the centre of the city — an area which had largely been developed in the second half of the 1930s. An attempt was therefore made to incorporate structural bays which would blend visually with neighbouring buildings, using a reinforced-concrete frame construction.

The interior is built around a travertine, skylighted hall. These skylights represent a further development of the type that was used in the library at Viipuri. Lighting fixtures are installed above the skylights over the hall so that the illumination at night will be the same as that by day and, also, in winter, serve to melt snow. The street façade is clad in copper and insulated with cork. The end elevation is in exposed brickwork.

Street front

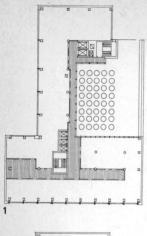

1

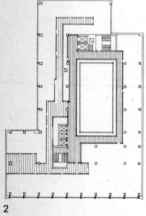

2

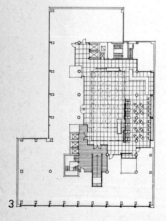

3

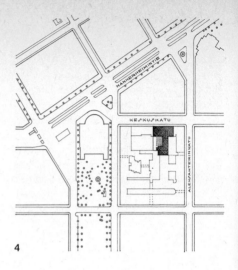

4

1 Plan of upper office floor
2 Plan at upper level of main
  hall
3 Plan at entrance level
4 Site plan
5 Longitudinal section
6 Detail of main hall showing
  skylights
7 Fountains in the main hall
8 General view of main hall

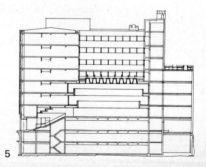

5

6

7

8

Architect's studio, Helsinki
Built 1955–1956

The studio was built in the garden city of Munkkiniemi, outside Helsinki, as an architectural office with two large drafting rooms, each with its own reception area, archives and conference room. Both are equal in size and scope, and can be used interchangeably for large or small projects.

The building has no windows overlooking the street, thus reducing disturbance from outside, while the back of the building faces an enclosed garden and amphitheatre which can be used for lectures, social occasions or recreation.

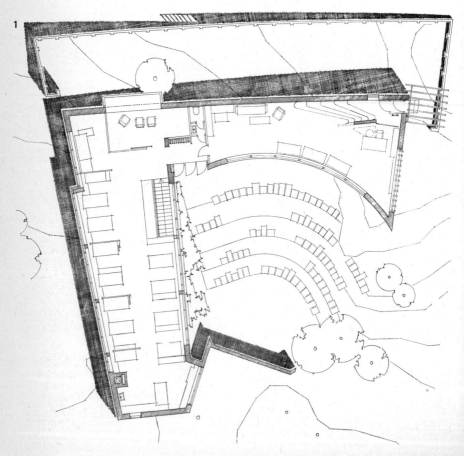

1

1 Plan of main floor
2 Interior of the curved studio
3 Large drafting room
4 The garden court, enclosed on three sides

Enso-Gutzeit headquarters building, Helsinki
Designed 1959   Built 1960—1962

The site for this building was in the old, Neo-Classical centre of the city. In this situation, the modern building marks a transition of architectural style, the architect's brief having been to design a modern structure which would harmonize with its surroundings.
The building stands on the Market Square, forming an axial termination of the Esplanade, and faces on to the harbour. (It thus has a similar architectural function to that of the Riva degli Schiavoni in Venice.)

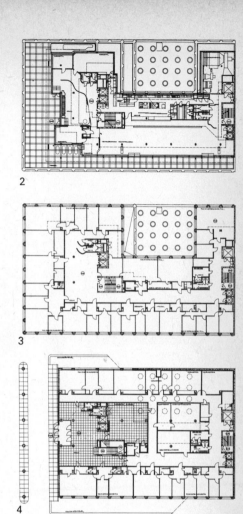

2

3

4

1 Detail of elevation
2 Plan at upper level
3 Typical floor-plan
4 Ground-floor-plan
5 Section

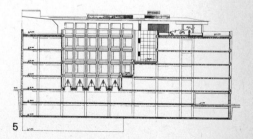

5

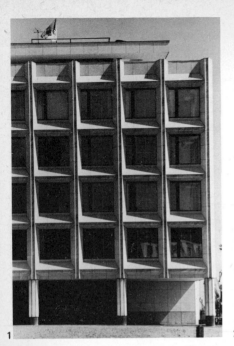

1 Detail of the entrance front
2 Rear elevation
3 General view from the harbour, with the Cathedral of St Nicholas beyond

Scandinavian Bank, Helsinki
Designed 1962   Built 1962–1964

This extension of the Scandinavian Bank is situated in an area containing buildings dating from the early part of the nineteenth century; on the Esplanade there are shops and office buildings from the beginning of the twentieth century; on Alexanderinkatu and in the imposing centre of the city the main feature is the Neo-Classical

1 Detail of elevation
2 View from the Esplanade
3 General view

Market Square, the central accent of which is the Cathedral of St Nicholas, designed by C. L. Engel. On the new bank building, the proportions and the design of the façades, clad in bronze, show an attempt to adapt this building to the different styles in the vicinity.

1 Plan of typical office floor
2 Plan at street entrance level
3 Colonnade at street level
4 Entrance foyer

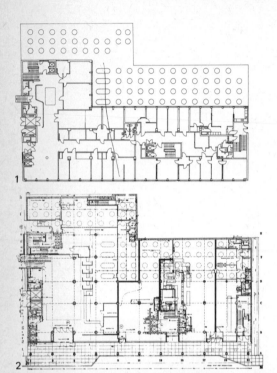

Academic Bookshop, Helsinki
Competition 1962   Built 1966–1969

The 'Kirjapalatsi' on the Keskuskatu (Central Street) and the Stockmann department store facing it were conceived as one unit. A pedestrian area and car parking are located beneath the street, with access via a ramp.

The main sales area of the bookshop, with its various departments, consists of a large hall with galleries above. Offices and administration are located on the five floors above.

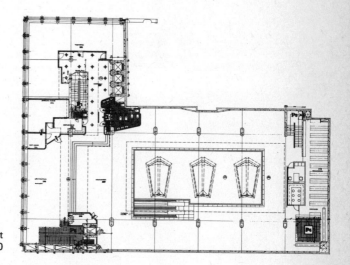

Plan of bookshop at first gallery level. Scale 1:650

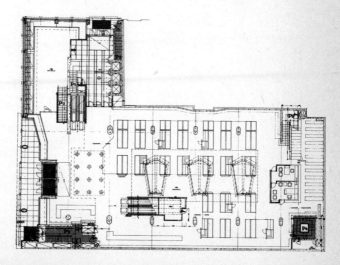

Plan at entrance level

135

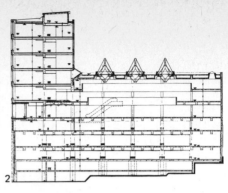

1 Exterior view
2 Longitudinal section
3 Main sales area, with galleries above

Ekenäs Savings Bank, Tammisaari
Designed 1964   Built 1965–1967

The bank with annexe for shops and offices constitutes the first stage of a residential and business centre in Tammisaari. Tammisaari, in Swedish, Ekenäs, is an old fishing village west of Helsinki. The old white frame houses, each with its separate garden, lend the village a charm of its own. The white houses form a contrast to the green of the many large trees, the dark sea and the blue sky.

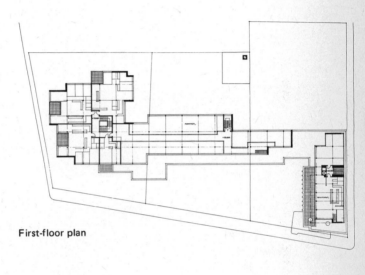

First-floor plan

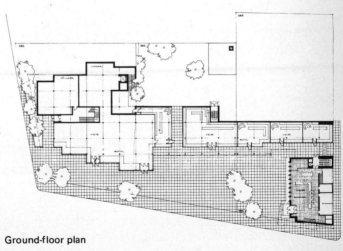

Ground-floor plan

1/2 Exterior views, showing the canopy over the entrance to the savings bank. Like all the nearby houses in the village, the new building was finished entirely in white

Factories

Cellulose Factory, Sunila
Designed 1935—1937   Built 1936—1939
Later extended 1951—1954

The Sunila cellulose combine in south Finland, not far from the port of Kotka, is
owned by five large industrial enterprises.
The contours of this rock island on which the factory is built have been left in their
natural form so that the production process starting on the highest level can step
down in its various individual stages to the level of the harbour. The centre of the
plan is built up into a terrace from which all phases of production can be observed.
The overall scheme also included workers' housing (see pp. 187—189).

Model of workers' housing and factory

This central area includes the administrative offices, laboratories etc., and the terrace also forms a garden providing a quiet zone for the administration separate from the factory buildings. Each of the various factory buildings is connected to the others by 'open-air corridors' in which the original trees have been left standing, thus retaining as far as possible the natural surroundings for the benefit of the employees. This separation of the individual factory buildings has made it possible to give each its own individual character, and the result is a pyramid-like complex rich in contrasts.

1 Site plan
2 General view with the stores on the left, the main plant and conveyor belt on the right
3 View of the factory

1

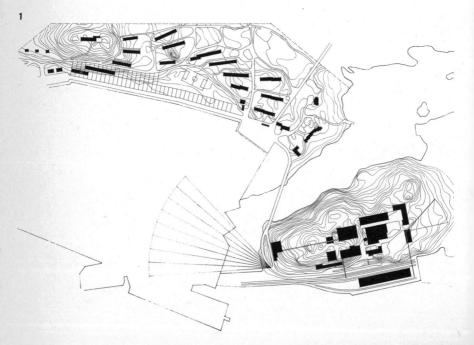

2

3

1 General view
2 The main plant, with the administrative buildings in the foreground
3 Detail of the buildings with natural landscape retained
4 Detail of rough-cast concrete wall

3

4

Sawmill, Varkaus
Designed and built 1945/46

The sawmill at Varkaus is one of the largest industrial concerns in Finland. The new mill, planned in its entirety to provide optimum output, was built on the site of an earlier industrial development and utilized existing concrete foundations; the structure itself consists of a light steel framework with timber cladding, adapted to functional needs.

1/2/3 External views, showing the use of vertical weather-boarding and the detailed shape of the building varying according to functional requirements

Heating plant for the Institute of Technology, Otaniemi
Designed 1962   Built 1962/63

This plant was designed to provide heat for all the buildings of the Institute (see pp. 83–88 and 109–112), and also to serve as a research laboratory for heating engineers. Later extensions have been carefully related to the design of the original building.

For maximum flexibility internally, a frame construction was chosen; the basement areas are of rough-cast concrete, and the external walls are faced with rough brick with copper facings above.

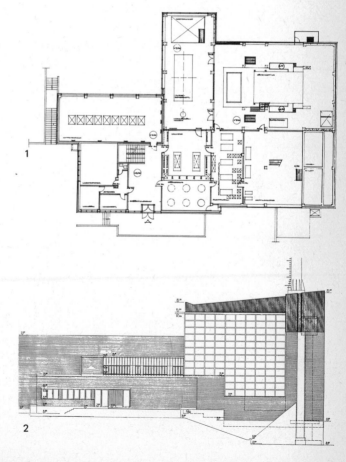

1 Ground-floor plan
2 Entrance elevation

1/2 Façade

Town Halls

Town Hall, Säynätsalo
Competition 1949   Built 1950—1952

Säynätsalo is a rugged island with a population of some 3,000; it is situated in Lake
Päjänne.
The town was laid out in 1945; shortly after the central market with the civic centre,
town hall and various commercial buildings were erected. The town hall complex
includes local government offices and a council chamber, together with a public
library, built around a central court. At ground-floor level there are also shops which
could be converted to local government use as the need for expansion arose.

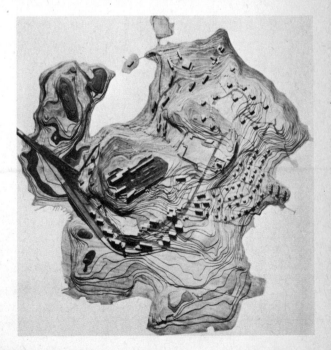

Model of the island

The council chamber is almost a cube. The triangulated timber trusses which support the secondary roof framing are fully exposed at ceiling level; this placing of the structural members in the room itself avoids the need for heavy built-in roof supports.

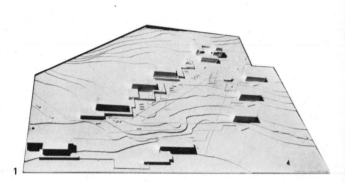

1

2

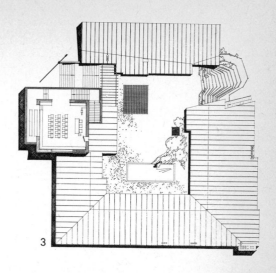

3

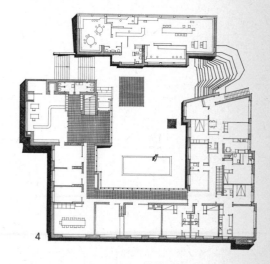

4

1 Model
2 View from the south-east, with
  the entrance stairs
3 Plan at roof level, with the council
  chamber at the left
4 Plan at main level
5 Section through library and
  administration wing

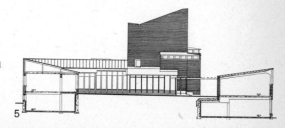

5

149

1 South front
2 Corridor serving offices
3 Main entrance

1

1 Ceiling of the council
  chamber seen from
  below
2 Detail of ceiling,
  showing roof trusses
3 Stairs on the west
  side leading to the
  court

2

3

Town Hall, Kiruna (Sweden)
Competition 1958   1st prize   Not built

Kiruna is the great 'gold mine' of Sweden, the site of open-cast iron workings from which ore with a high iron content is mined. This project attempted to exploit the exceptional environment.

The town hall and communal building would have a view over the dramatic landscape created by the slag heaps resulting from the extraction of iron from the ore — completely in keeping with the special character of the whole region. The town hall was designed in such a way that the enormous snowdrifts that occur here would fall automatically from the building onto the almost windowless north side.

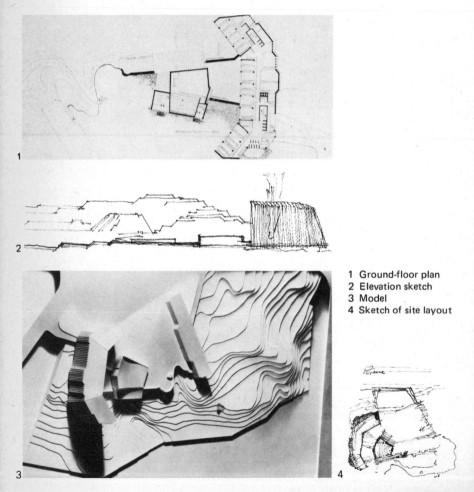

1 Ground-floor plan
2 Elevation sketch
3 Model
4 Sketch of site layout

Town Hall, Seinäjoki
Designed 1961/62   Built 1963–1965

The town hall, together with the already built church (see p. 161) and library, forms part of the overall plan for the civic centre (see pp. 9, 10). The council chamber — the dominant visual accent of this building — is especially remarkable for its high roof with skylights. A staircase flanked by shrubbery and fountains connects the main square with this building complex. The main entrance to the administrative offices is below the level of the council chamber which, however, also has its own access via the staircase.

1 The main approach to the town hall
2 View of the council chamber and municipal offices from the north-east

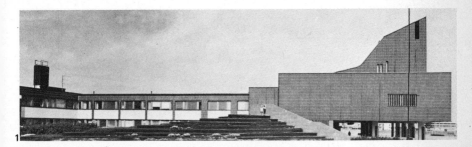

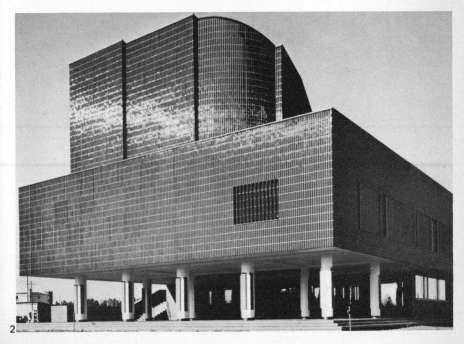

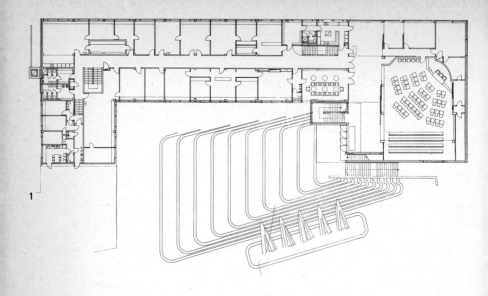

1 Plan at upper level showing offices and
  council chamber. Scale 1:700
2 East elevation
3 Interior of the council chamber
  showing skylights

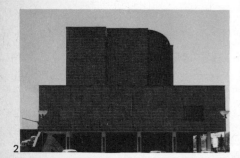

Alajärvi Town Hall
Designed 1966   Built 1967—1969

Alajärvi is a small town with a population of about 5,000, in west central Finland.
The project consisted of a town hall and health centre, together with a separate
community centre, the whole embracing an inner pedestrian zone. The new buildings
are intended to blend with the surroundings, which include the nearby neo-classical
church, retaining as far as possible the rural character of the place.

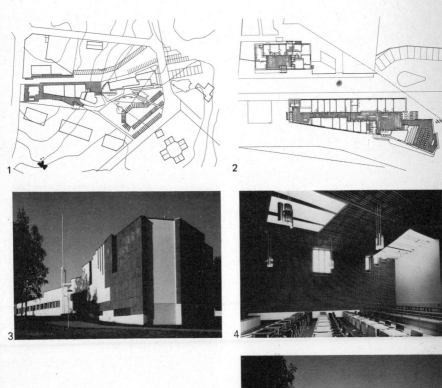

1 Site plan
2 Ground-floor plan. Scale 1:2,400
3 Exterior view with the council chamber
  in the foreground
4 The interior of the council chamber
5 Entrance elevation

Churches

Malm Funeral Chapels, Helsinki
Competition 1950   1st prize   Not built

The architectural principles governing the design of this complex of three funeral
chapels were based on the need for absolute simplicity and the avoidance of
distracting details.
Bearing in mind the emotional overtones of funerals, the architect planned the layout
of the three chapels in such a way that each would have its own approach and formal
entrance. In this way, even when all three chapels were in use simultaneously, privacy
would be assured for any one group of mourners.

1

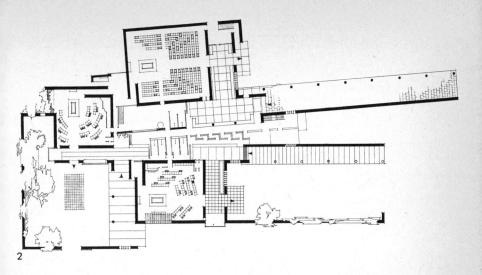

2

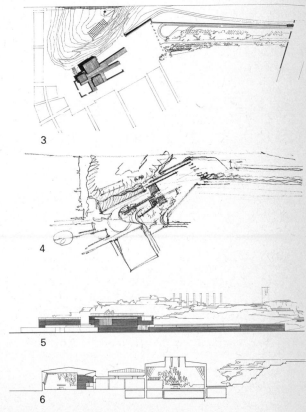

3

4

5

6

1 Model
2 Ground-floor plan
3 Site plan
4 Early design sketch
5 Longitudinal section
6 Cross-section

Cemetery and Funeral Chapel, Lyngby (Denmark)
Competition 1952   Not built

In this competition for a cemetery with funeral chapel, the programme stated that
the chapel would be used for up to 15 funerals per day. As he was unable to reconcile
himself with the idea of 'mass-production' methods in relation to funeral practice,
Aalto's design provided for three chapels instead of one. In this way it would be
possible for several funerals to proceed simultaneously, with separate entrance courts
for groups of mourners.
The cemetery lies in a crater-like ravine. All paths to the graves lead down this ravine.
Paralleling the paths are water courses flowing in small brooks.
Every means has been employed here to seek a solution that would provide each
individual funeral with an atmosphere of peace and privacy.

1 Site plan
2 Sketch design

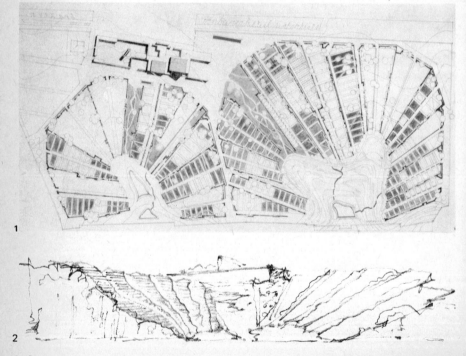

1

2

158

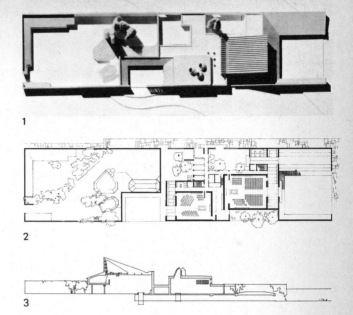

1

2

3

1 Model seen from above
2 Ground-floor plan
3 Longitudinal section
4 Model

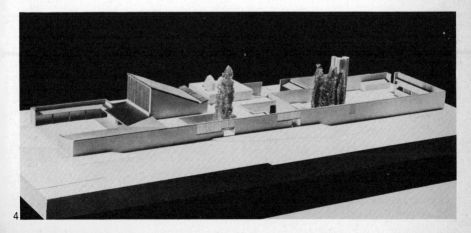

4

Church, Lahti
Competition 1950   Redesigned 1970

A competition for the principal church in the town of Lahti, about 60 miles north-east of Helsinki, was held in 1950, but the plan was not executed and the present scheme is basically new.

The site is a rising triangular plot between two main thoroughfares in the centre of the town; the elevated site and the prominent church tower would combine to make the building the dominant visual accent of the town. The body of the church is a cube-like mass, above which soars the tower composed of individual columnar elements.

1 Site plan
2 Model
3 Entrance elevation
4 Ground-floor plan

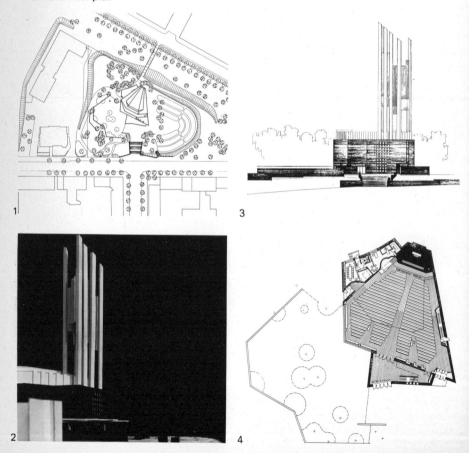

Church and Parish Hall, Seinäjoki
Church: Competition 1952   Built 1958–1960
Parish hall: Designed 1963   Built 1964–1966

Seinäjoki is the episcopal see for central and northern Finland, and the church and parish hall form part of the urban scheme for the civic centre (see pp. 9, 10). The church square is used for open-air worship and for large-scale celebrations at festival times. The free-standing belfry and clock tower provides a landmark, and from its top there are extensive views over the sea and the surrounding countryside.
The parish hall is built around the square which rises from the level of the church site. Part of the roof of the parish hall forms an open terrace.

1 Ground-floor plan. Scale 1:1,300
2 The free-standing belfry

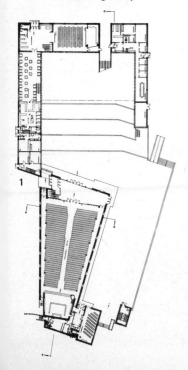

1 Interior, looking across the nave
2 The organ gallery above the entrance
3 Side chapel with stained-glass window
4 Entrance vestibule
5 Side elevation of church and tower
6 The church and presbytery seen from the town hall (foreground; see p. 153)

Church in Vuoksenniska, Imatra
Designed 1956   Built 1957–1959

The church in Vuoksenniska is one of three serving the community of Imatra. The
setting — characterized by many industrial buildings all around — was an important
factor in the design chosen.

The bell-tower presented a special difficulty in this respect, owing to the presence of
many tall factory chimneys in the immediate surroundings. Form, rather than height,
was therefore important in achieving a clear visual distinction from a distance.

The external form of the building reflects the internal sub-divisions, based on the need
for spaces for social as well as religious purposes. Partitions are used to separate the
three main parts, and these can be removed when necessary to form a single church
space to accommodate up to 800 people. With the partitions in position, the church
can seat a congregation of 290. Other smaller rooms are located at the western end
of the building and can be reached by separate entrances.

The asymmetrical arrangement of the interior was inspired by the liturgy of the
Lutheran service. The wall on the pulpit side in straight, and the opposite longitudinal
wall is — for acoustic reasons — planned in three curved sections. The asymmetry is
also apparent in the vertical plane, with the windows in the curving wall arranged in
a sloping, diagonal pattern. Together with the ceiling on this side of the church, they
form an acoustic reflecting board. In order to test the acoustic effects before construction, empirical studies were made in the architect's studio with the aid of models.

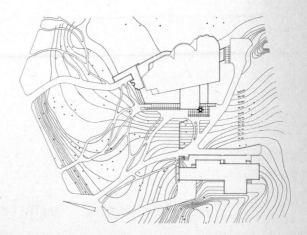

Site plan

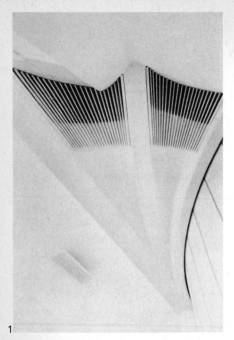

1 Slots in the ceiling for heating and ventilation
2 Detail of curved wall and canted windows
3 View of the organ
4 Longitudinal section with organ
5 Plan at organ loft level, showing internal subdivisions
6 The church proper, consisting of three sub-divisible areas. The 16-inch thick concrete partition walls provide complete acoustic separation when in position

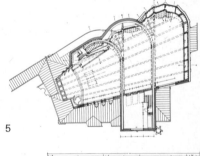

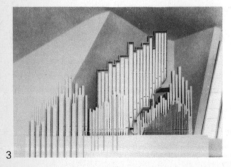

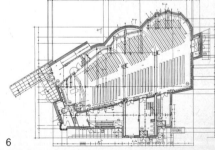

1 Exterior view showing the form of the three internal sub-divisions
2 View of the altar, pulpit and organ
3 Detail of design sketch
4 General view, with the pastor's house in the right foreground; the walls are finished in white stucco and the roof is copper

Parish Centre, Wolfsburg (Germany)
Designed 1959   Built 1960—1962

The church buildings are situated in the middle of a residential development on the
edge of a green-belt area. The group consists of three separate buildings. The church
and parish hall are disposed around a square and thus constitute the principal element;
the third building includes accommodation for the clergy and clubrooms and facilities
for young people. The square is closed off on the side facing on to the road and on
this side stands the open belfry. The church square is connected to the adjacent park
by a narrow passageway.

1 Site plan
2/3 Exterior views

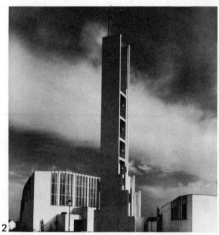

1

2

3

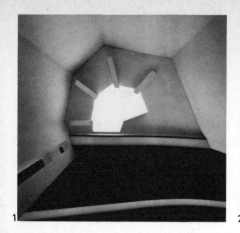

1 The skylight seen from below
2 The rear of the church seen from the altar
3 Longitudinal section
4 Interior view of church windows
5 Exterior detail of windows

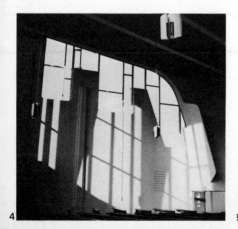

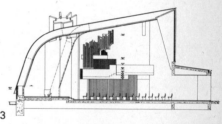

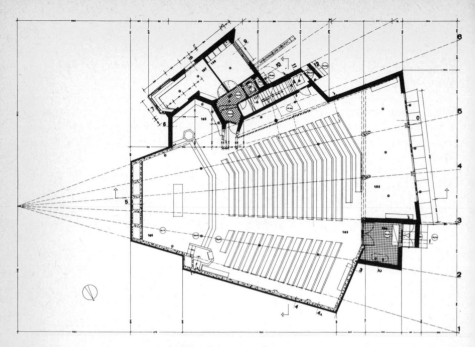

Church plan and view from the side entrance towards altar and pulpit

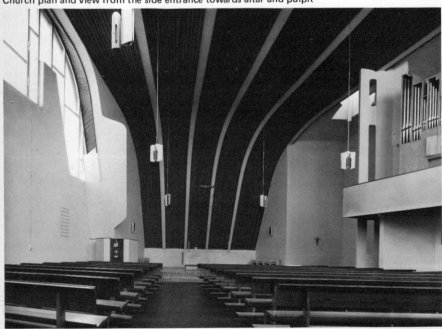

Parish Centre, Detmerode (Germany)
Designed 1963   Built 1965–1968

Detmerode is the latest residential suburb to be created for the industrial town of Wolfsburg.
The church has permanent seating for a congregation of 250 people, and the additional empty space customary in German churches can be filled with chairs to accommodate a maximum of over 600 people. The ceiling has domed wooden acoustic reflectors, each about eight feet in diameter. There is a small chapel in the basement beneath the choir.

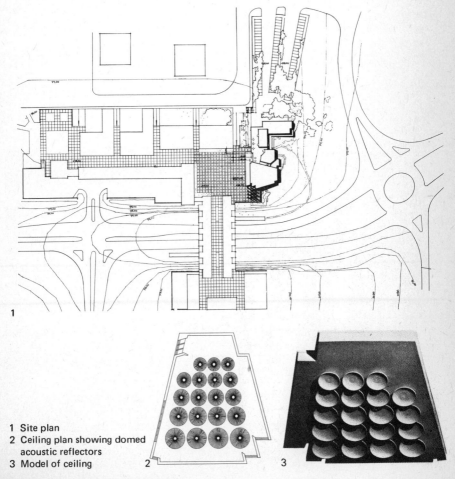

1

1 Site plan
2 Ceiling plan showing domed
   acoustic reflectors
3 Model of ceiling   2   3

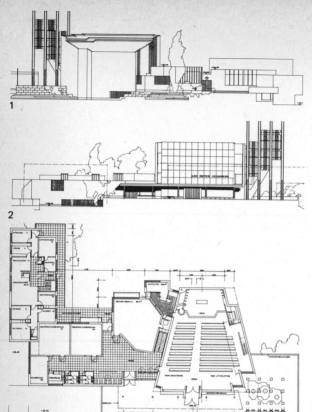

1 Rear elevation
2 Entrance elevation
3 Plan at main floor level
4 Belfry
5 Cross-section

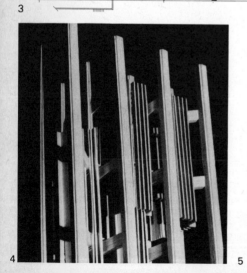

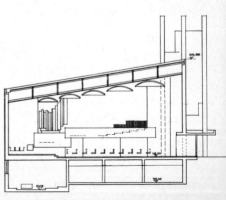

Riola Parish Centre, Bologna (Italy)
Designed 1966   Under construction

The new centre is situated on an old road leading into the city, bounded on one side
by the river Reno and on the other by an ancient Roman bridge. The new church was
one of the first in which the 'reformed' Roman Catholic liturgy would be given
expression in architectural terms; the aim was to provide a close relationship between
altar, choir and organ, as well as the baptistery. The shape of the church itself is an
asymmetrical basilica with asymmetrical vaulting through which light, directed
especially towards the altar, enters the building. Galleries were dispensed with,
but the choir area was extended to compensate for their absence.
The front wall of the church can be opened so that the forecourt serves as an
extension to it.

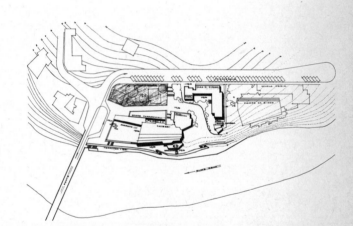

Site plan

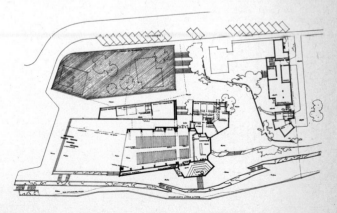

Plan at ground level.
Scale 1:1,500

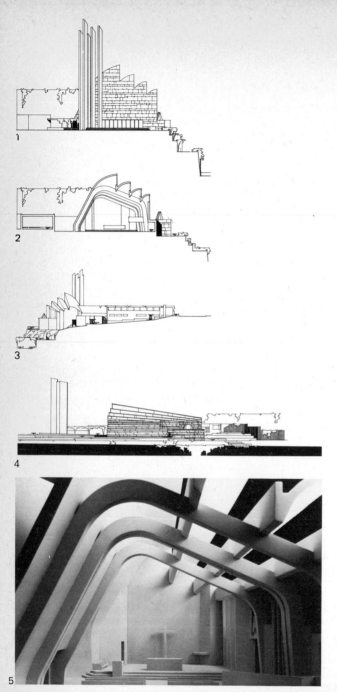

1 Entrance façade
2 Cross-section
3 Lateral façade
4 Longitudinal façade
  from the river with
  embankment
5 Model of the church

Family Houses

Architect's House, Munksnäs, Helsinki
Designed 1934   Built 1935/36

Planned originally as a combined house and office, the building is now used as a
private house and studio, following the completion of the architect's later office
building (see pp. 128, 129). The materials used were tubular steel filled with concrete,
with exterior walls of whitewashed brick; wood was used for the interior partition
walls. The terrace at the upper level serves as a roof garden between the living and
studio areas.

Garden façade

1 Entrance court
2 Roof terrace
3 Ground-floor plan
4 Plan at upper level

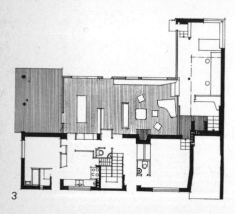

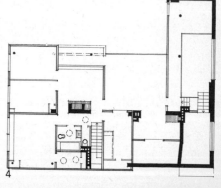

Villa Mairea, Noormarkku
Designed 1937/38   Built 1938/39

The Villa Mairea was built as a country house for the architect's friends Maire and
Harry Gullichsen. The house stands in the middle of a pine forest at the top of a hill
in western Finland. The house looks out mainly on to continuous unbroken stretches
of forest, with a narrow vista through an opening in the trees on to a river and
sawmill (which at the time of the house's construction was one of the first industrial
enterprises in this part of Finland).
Although the inner court is open on one side, the forest creates an effective 'wall'
enclosing it. A sauna and swimming pool are located on the opposite side from
the large living room on the ground floor; the sauna wing is of Finnish fir, and the
balconies and parts of the exterior of the house are clad in teak.

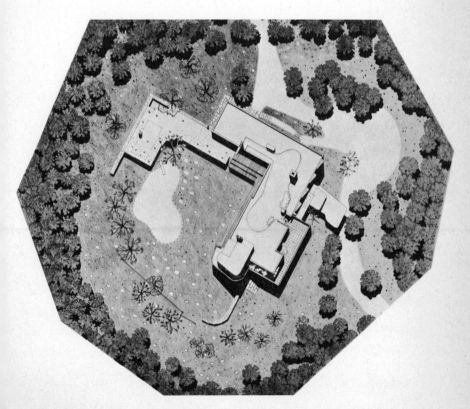

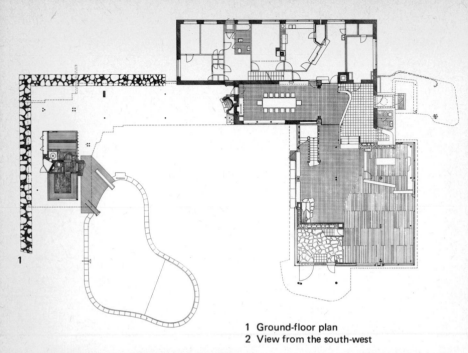

1 Ground-floor plan
2 View from the south-west

1 View from the south
2 Main entrance

1 Detail of exterior, showing different uses of wood in wall cladding and balconies
2 View from the entrance looking into the hall
3 Plan at upper level
4 Sitting area in the living room, with view of forest trees

1 Fireplace in the hall
2 View from the hall towards the sauna
3 Swimming pool and sauna

1 Swimming pool and sauna
2 The wall of the sauna

Architect's Summerhouse, Muuratsalo
Designed and built 1953

The summerhouse was designed and built not only as a place to live and work, but also as a practical test of a variety of materials and techniques. Located in the lake country of north central Finland, the house consists of two wings at right angles, one containing the living areas and the other the bedrooms. A square court is formed by enclosing the other two sides with high walls. The exterior walls within this court have a mosaic-like appearance, since they are divided into some fifty areas in which different types and sizes of bricks and ceramic tiles are used with various methods of jointing, in order to test their effect from both the aesthetic and the practical standpoint. The house has a lean-to roof rising steeply over the living area towards the west wall.

View from the landing stage

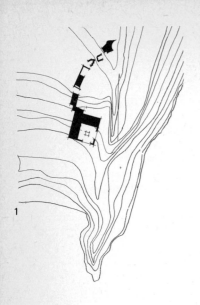

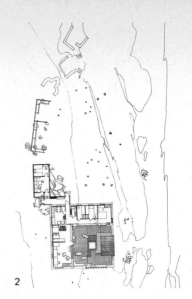

1 Site plan
2 Ground-floor plan
3 View of the court

1/2 Details of external walls in the court,
showing use of different brick and
ceramic tile finishes

1

2

183

Maison Carré, Bazoches-sur-Guyonne (France)
Built 1956–1959

The house was built for Louis Carré, a well-known art-dealer. The brief called for a family house with hanging space for paintings, while avoiding the appearance of an art gallery. The architect was also required to design the internal details throughout, including furnishings, lamps, fabrics etc., and to plan and design the garden surrounding the house. The house stands at the top of a hill, and has extensive views all around. Internally, it was necessary to vary ceiling heights in order to provide both window and skylight illumination of areas of wall space. Each of the main rooms leads directly on to its own patio.

The upper part of the exterior is brickwork painted white, and the lower part is grey travertine. The roof is of copper and natural slate.

1 Sketch of the living-room elevation
2 Site plan
3 Ground-floor plan showing: (right) the living room; (centre) entrance hall; (left) dining room and service rooms; (above) bedrooms

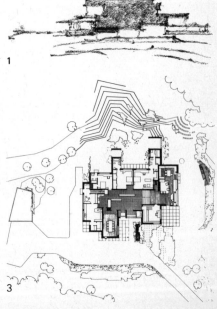

1

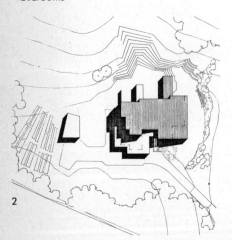

2

3

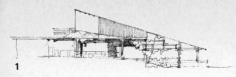

1

2

3

1 Sketch of entrance elevation
2 West elevation, showing the high windows
  of the vaulted entrance hall
3 Bedroom wing
4 Guest rooms
5 South elevation
6 Living room porch

6

4

5

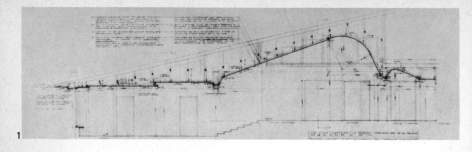

1 Working drawing of the ceiling to the entrance hall and living room
2 Entrance hall with vaulted ceiling, view into living room
3 Lamp
4 Living room
5 Dining room

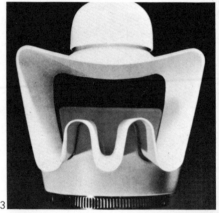

Apartment Blocks and High-Rise Buildings

Workers' Housing, Sunila
Designed 1935—1937   Built 1936—1939

The housing for employees of the Sunila Cellulose Factory was built in conjunction with the industrial buildings (see p. 139). The site was a tree-covered area with numerous rocky outcrops and small valleys. The overall plan was based on the stipulation that only the south slopes should be used for dwellings, with the valleys serving as pathways and gardens, while the pine forest on the north slopes should remain undisturbed.

1 Site plan
2 Plan of typical terraced apartments
3 Terraced apartment building (without balconies)

Various grades of housing were designed, some with gardens for supervisory staff. The residential development was built in five stages. Each stage called for the installation of a district heating system, water mains and sewerage. Heating is supplied from one plant for three housing blocks treated as one unit.

Within the overall development there are distinct independent housing groups, each with its own stylistic characteristics. As each stage succeeded the previous one, new features were introduced and alterations made in the light of experience already gained from the earlier buildings.

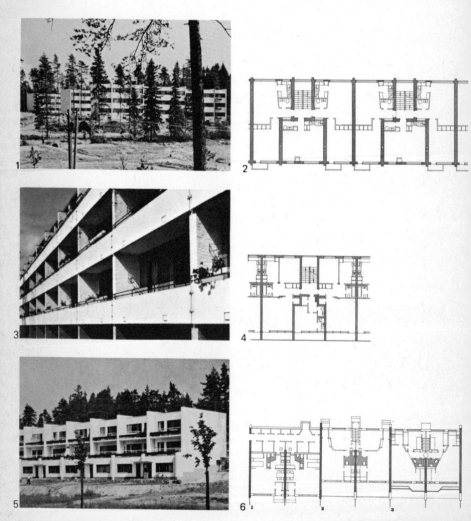

1 General view of a housing block; three such
  blocks constitute one unit for central heating
  and hot-water supply
2 Plan of typical apartments
3 Housing block with larger balconies
4 Plan of apartment
5 Terraced housing with three apartments per
  unit; owing to the slope of the site stairs
  were not necessary for every apartment
6 Plan of typical apartments
7 Cross-section of apartments
8 Exterior view of three-storey apartment house
9 Floor plan of housing for supervisory staff
10 Housing for supervisory staff, showing
   staggered arrangement with fan-shaped walled
   gardens

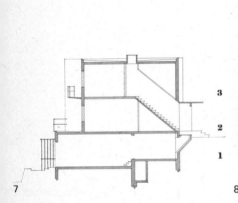

7

3

2

1

8

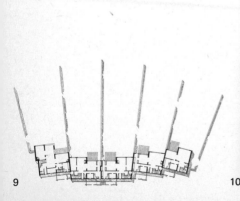

9

10

Terraced houses, Kauttua
Designed 1937   Built 1938–1940

This project presented an opportunity to develop the housing type, first seen in the workers' housing at Sunila, a stage further. The site was characterized by steep slopes covered with pine forest. The southern slopes were used for residential development, and in this case the steepness of these slopes dictated a vertical, stepped treatment following the natural contours of the site.

Site plan

190

The structural design which resulted was completely free of stairs, even though the terrace consisted of five storeys. Access from each dwelling to its 'basement' area could also be arranged in the same manner since the basement was built into the side of the hill at the same level as the living accommodation. The roof of the lower dwelling also acted as a terrace for the one immediately above it.

1 Isometric drawing
2 Cross-section showing use of sloping site
3 Entrance elevation seen through the
   pine forest
4 South elevation

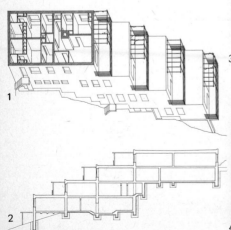

Apartment building, Hansaviertel, Berlin
Designed and built 1955—1957

The model apartment building in the Hansaviertel was built on the occasion of the Interbau exhibition in Berlin. This design sought to combine as far as possible the advantages of the private house with its own garden and those of the typical apartment house. Hence, conventional narrow balconies were expanded to become outdoor patios around which the rooms of each apartment were grouped. This 'intimate arrangement' gives the occupants the advantage of a small garden combined with complete privacy.

The south façade

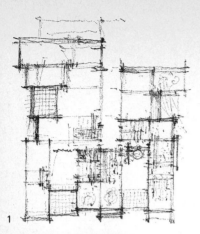

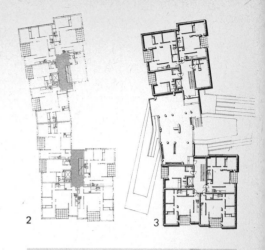

1 Design sketch
2 Typical floor plan
3 Floor plan at
   entrance level
4/5 Conceptual model of
   the 'patio apartment'
6 East elevation

1 Ceiling decoration in the hall
2 Model apartment with furniture made by the Artek company
3 Interior of the entrance portico which can also be used for outdoor social gatherings
4 View from the dining area towards the living room and balcony

'Neue Vahr' apartment building, Bremen (Germany)
Designed 1958   Built 1959–1962

The fan-like plan was conceived so that the very small one-room apartments would benefit from a broader outlook through the larger windows which this arrangement makes possible. Access to all apartments is by lift only, thus reducing the amount of space required for movement on any one floor to a minimum.

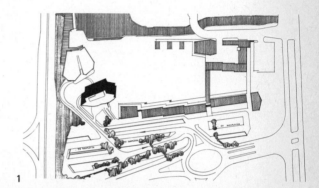

1 Site plan
2 West elevation

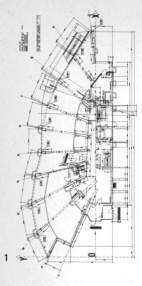
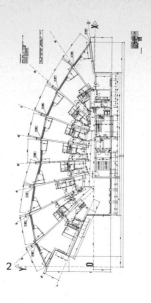

1

2

3

1 Ground-floor plan
2 Typical floor plan
3 Preliminary design of typical floor plan
4 South elevation
5 Detail of façade

4

5

'Schönbühl' apartment building, Lucerne (Switzerland)
Designed 1965   Built 1966–1968

The Schönbühl high-rise apartment building is a development of the Neue Vahr block in Bremen. The principal difference between the two buildings is that in Lucerne an attempt was made to accommodate apartments of more than two rooms in a fan-like arrangement. For reasons of economy, the maximum number of apartments possible

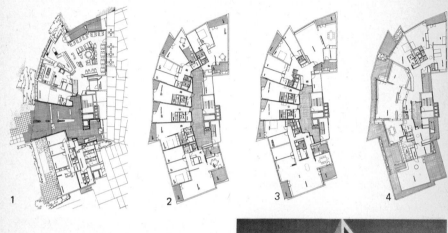

1
2
3
4

1 Ground-floor plan
2 Typical floor plan
3 Fourteenth-floor plan
4 Plan at roof level
5 View from the south, showing the
   fan-shaped east façade, and access to
   shopping centre on the west side

5

was planned for each floor. All the apartments are served by a common staircase and one group of lifts, with the individual entrances radiating off a hallway or service area at each level; the communal part of the building is thus reduced to a minimum and in turn gives rise to the fan shape of the layout and reduces disturbance. The broken-up appearance of the main façade is caused by the varying sizes of the apartments.

1 View of model, showing the adjacent shopping centre planned by Professor A. Roth
2 Restaurant
3 North and west façades, seen from the car park on the roof of the shopping centre
4 Interior of a living room with furniture made by the Artek company

Furniture

Furniture and Lamps

'In order to achieve practical goals and valid aesthetic forms in connection with architecture, one cannot always start from a rational and technical standpoint — perhaps even never. Human imagination must have free room in which to unfold.

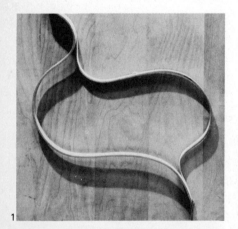

1–3 Experimental designs in wood

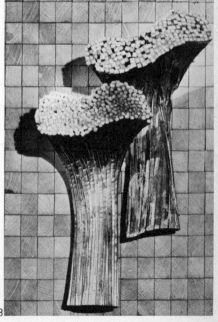

This was usually the case with my experiments in wood. Purely playful forms, with no practical function whatsoever, have, in some cases, led to a practical form only after ten years had elapsed.

The first experiments consisted of trying to bend laminated structures in one direction. It was always my dream to know how to create multi-dimensional, sculptural forms in wood, which could eventually lead to freer and more stable forms.

The first attempt to construct organic form-volumes of wood without the use of cutting techniques led to triangular solutions, considering the orientation of the wood fibres.'

A.A.

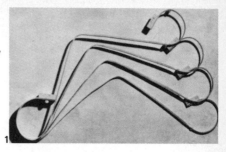

1

2

The first light standardized wood furniture was developed for the Paimio Sanatorium, not just as a protest against the cold properties of tubular steel furniture, but rather with the specific goal of using material better suited to the requirements of the human body. An experimental workshop was set up with a local lumber firm and soon the first experiments were undertaken with bent and pressed wood.

The purpose of these experiments was to develop light, washable and hygienic chairs, which, thanks to the natural springiness of the material, would also be comfortable to sit on. In the first series of furniture designs tubular steel was also included, but only in such a way that steel parts were never in contact with the human body. Later came the bent wood designs. One of the first attempts to render wood elastic consisted of bending the wood in such a way that, under load, each radius of a curvilinear form tended to become shorter, with the result that the glued plywood layers became compressed. The material used was local birch wood, and the conventional techniques for bending wood, e.g. steaming etc., were not employed — only the natural moisture content of the wood was used.

With Paimio began the pursuit of interior design, which, still today, continues with the Artek company. Similar agreements with the building committee made it possible to develop not only furniture, but also lighting fixtures, smaller accessories and other specially designed components as well.

1/2 Experimental forms in wood
3/4/5 A selection of chair designs

3

4

5

1—6 Lamps and glass bowl

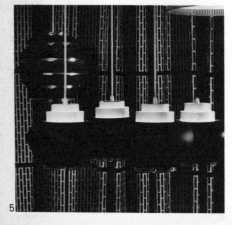

Chronological List of Projects and Buildings

First date is year of design or beginning of construction; second date is year of completion of projects executed or of planning stage.

1918	House of the Architect's Parents, Alajärvi, Remodelling
1918	Belfry, Kauhajärvi
1921/22	Building for Associations of Patriots, Seinäjoki
1922	Industrial Exhibition, Tampere
1922/23	Two-Family House, Jyväskylä
1923	Workers' Club, Jyväskylä, Competition, 1st Prize
1923/24	Apartment Building, Jyväskylä
1923—25	Workers' Club, Jyväskylä
1924	Church, Aeänekoski, Restoration
1924	Church, Anttola, Restoration
1925	Post Office, Jyväskylä
1925	Building for Associations of Patriots, Jyväskylä, Competition, 2nd Prize
1925	Church, Jämsä, Competition
1925	Church, Viitasaari, Remodelling
1926—29	Church, Muurame
1927	Töölö Church, Helsinki, Competition
1927	Viinikka Church, Tampere, Competition, 2nd Prize
1927	Pylkönmäki Church, Restoration, Belfry
1927	Municipal Library, Viipuri, Competition, 1st Prize
1927/28	Standard Apartment Building, Turku
1927—29	Farmers' Co-operative Building and Finnish Theatre, Turku
1927—29	Building for Associations of Patriots, Jyväskylä
1927—29	Turun Sanomat Newspaper Office, Turku*
1928	Tuberculosis Sanatorium, Paimio, Competition, 1st Prize
1928	Aitta Summer Houses, Competition, 1st Prize
1928	Church, Korpilahti, Restoration
1929	Church, Kemijärvi, Restoration
1929	Turku 700th Anniversary Exhibition*
1929—33	Tuberculosis Sanatorium, Paimio*
1930	Institute for Physical Education, Vierumäki, Competition, 3rd Prize
1930	Michele Agricola Church, Helsinki, Competition
1930	Stadium and Sports Centre, Helsinki, Competition
1930	University Hospital, Zagreb, Yugoslavia, Competition
1930/31	Cellulose Factory, Toppila, Oulu
1930—35	Municipal Library, Viipuri *
1932	Helsinki Stadium, Competition
1932	Prefabricated One-Family House, Competition
1932	Enso-Gutzeit Week-End Cabin, Competition
1933	Housing for Employees of the Sanatorium, Paimio*
1933	Terraced Housing for Doctors of the Sanatorium, Paimio*
1933	Redevelopment Plan for Norrmalm, Stockholm, Sweden, Competition*
1934	Railway Station, Tampere, Competition
1934	Stenius Housing Development, Munkkiniemi
1934	Exhibition Pavilion, Helsinki, Competition, 3rd Prize
1934—36	Architect's Own House, Munkkiniemi*
1935	Finnish Pavilion at the Paris World's Fair Competition, 1st and 2nd Prize
1935—39	Cellulose Factory, Sunila, 1st stage of construction*
1936	Art Museum, Tallinn, Estonia, Competition*
1936/37	Finnish Pavilion at the Paris World's Fair*

1937	Savoy Restaurant, Helsinki
1937	Development at Kauttua, Competition
1937	Nordic United Bank, Karhula
1937	Finnish Pavilion at the New York World's Fair, Competition, 1st, 2nd and 3rd Prize
1937/38	Director's House, Sunila
1937/38	Two-Storey Housing, Sunila*
1937/38	Two-Storey Terrace Housing, Sunila, 1st group*
1937/38	Two-Storey Terrace Housing, Sunila, 2nd group*
1937—39	Villa Mairea, Noormarkku*
1937—40	Terraced Housing, Kauttua*
1938	Forestry Pavilion at the Agricultural Exhibition, Lapua
1938	Blomberg Film Studio, Westend, Helsinki, Competition
1938	Extension of the University Library, Helsinki, Competition, 2nd Prize
1938	Anjala Paper Factory, Inkeroinen
1938/39	Three-Storey Terraced Housing, Sunila, 1st group*
1938/39	Finnish Pavilion at the New York World's Fair*
1938/39	Three-Storey Terrace Housing, Sunila, 2nd group*
1938/39	Elementary School, Inkeroinen
1938/39	Anjala Apartment Buildings, Inkeroinen, 1st group
1938/39	Anjala Terrace Housing, Inkeroinen, 2nd group
1938/39	Housing for Engineers, Anjala, Inkeroinen
1939—45	Ahlström Apartment Buildings, Karhula
1940	Haka Housing Development, Helsinki, Competition
1940	Traffic Plan and Design of Erottaia Square, Helsinki, Competition, 1st Prize
1941	Plan for an Experimental Town
1941/42	Regional Plan for the Kokemäki Valley
1942—46	Urban Design Project for Säynätsalo
1942/43	Women's Dormitory, Kauttua
1943	Town Centre, Oulu, Competition
1943	Merikoski Power Station, Oulu, Competition
1944	Town Centre, Avesta, Sweden, Competition
1944	Strömberg Housing Development, Vaasa
1944	Extension to Factory, Kauttua
1944/45	Urban Design Project for Rovaniemi
1944/45	Ahlström Mechanical Workshop, Karhula
1944—47	Strömberg Meter Factory, Vaasa
1944—47	Strömberg Terrace Housing, Vaasa
1945	Engineer's House, Kauttua
1945	Sauna, Kauttua
1945	Artek Exhibition Pavilion, Hedemora, Sweden
1945/46	Sawmill, Varkaus, Extension*
1945/46	One-Family Housing Development, Varkaus
1946	Heimdal Housing Development, Nynäshamn, Sweden, Competition
1946	Master Plan, Nynäshamn, Sweden, Competition
1946	One-Family House, Pihlava
1946	Sauna for the Villa Mairea, Noormarkku
1947	Strömberg Sauna and Laundry, Vaasa
1947	Johnson Research Institute, Avesta, Sweden
1947/48	Baker House, Massachusetts Institute of Technology Senior Dormitory, Cambridge Cambridge (Mass.), USA*
1947—53	Regional Plan for Imatra*
1948	Forum redivivum, Cultural and Administrative Centre, Helsinki, Competition, 1st Prize
1949	Ahlström Factory Warehouse, Karhula
1949	General Plan of the Institute of Technology, Otaniemi, Competition, 1st Prize
1949	Town Hall, Säynätsalo, Competition, 1st Prize

1949/50	Tampella Housing, Tampere
1950	Church, Lahti, Competition, 1st Prize
1950	Malm Funeral Chapels, Helsinki, Competition, 1st Prize*
1950	Kivelä Hospital, Helsinki, Competition
1950	College of Education, Jyväskylä, Competition, 1st Prize
1950—52	Gymnasium, Otaniemi*
1950—52	Town Hall, Säynätsalo*
1950—55	Regional Plan for Lappland
1951	Erottaja Pavilion, Helsinki
1951	Regional Theatre, Kuopio, Competition, 1st Prize
1951	Enso-Gutzeit Paper Factory, Kotka
1951	One-Family House, Oulu
1951	Worker's Housing, Inkeroinen
1951	Rautatalo Office Building, Helsinki, Competition, 1st Prize
1951/52	Typpi OY Sulphate Factory, Oulu
1951/52	Apartment Building for Employees of the Typpi OY, Oulu
1951—53	Enso-Gutzeit Paper Mill, Summa
1951—54	Paper Mill, Chandraghona, Pakistan
1951—54	Cellulose Factory, Sunila, 2nd stage of construction*
1951—54	Three-Storey Apartment House, Sunila, 3rd group*
1952	Cemetery and Funeral Chapel, Kongens Lyngby, Copenhagen, Denmark, Competition, 2nd Prize*
1952	Building of the Association of Finnish Engineers, Helsinki
1952	Enso-Gutzeit Country Club, Kallvik
1952	Church, Seinäjoki, Competition, 1st Prize
1952—54	Housing for the Personnel of the National Pensions Institute, Munkkiniemi
1953	Sports and Concert Centre Vogelweidplatz, Vienna, Austria, Competition, 1st Prize
1953	Imatra Centre Design Project
1953	Architect's Summer House, Muuratsalo*
1953—55	Rautatalo Office Building, Helsinki*
1953—56	College of Education, Jyväskylä*
1953—56	Architect's Studio, Munkkiniemi*
1954	Studio R. S., Como, Italy
1954	Sports Hall for the Institute of Technology, Otaniemi
1954	Housing AERO, Helsinki
1955	Urban Design Project for Summa
1955	Bank Building Baghdad, Iraq, Competition
1955	Theatre and Concert Hall, Oulu
1955—57	Apartment Building in the Hansaviertel Berlin, Germany*
1955—57	Town Hall, Göteborg, Sweden, Competition, 1st Prize
1955—58	Kultuuritalo, Helsinki*
1955—64	Main Building of the Institute of Technology, Otaniemi*/**
1956	Main Railway Station 'Drottning Troget', Göteborg, Sweden, Competition, 1st Prize
1956	Director's House (Typpi OY), Oulu
1956	General Plan of the University of Oulu
1956	Finnish Pavilion at the Biennale, Venice, Italy
1956—58	Church, Vuoksenniska, Imatra*
1956—59	Villa Louis Carré, Bazoches, Ile-de-France, France*
1957	Town Hall, Marl, Germany, Competition
1957—61	Korkalovaara Housing Development, Rovaniemi
1957—61	Sundh Centre, Avesta, Sweden
1958	Town Hall, Kiruna, Sweden, Competition, 1st Prize*
1958	Museum, Aalborg, Denmark, Competition, 1st Prize*
1958	Museum, Baghdad, Iraq
1958	Building of the Post Office Administration, Baghdad, Iraq

1958	Kampementsbacken Housing Development, Stockholm, Sweden, Competition 1st Prize*
1958—60	Church, Seinäjoki**
1958—62	'Neue Vahr' High-Rise Apartment Block, Bremen, Germany*/**
1958—62	Cultural Centre, Wolfsburg, Germany, Competition*/**
1959	Opera House in Essen, Germany, Competition, 1st Prize*
1959	Björnholm Housing Development, Helsinki*
1959	Urban Centre, Seinäjoki, Competition, 1st Prize*/**
1959—62	Central Finnish Museum, Jyväskylä**
1959—62	Headquarters of Enso-Gutzeit, Helsinki*/**
1959—62	Parish Centre Wolfsburg, Germany**
1959—64	City Centre, Helsinki*/**
1960	Finnish War Memorial, Suomussalmi
1960/61	Shopping Centre, Otaniemi
1960—63	Lieksankoski Power Station, Lieksa
1960—63	Thermotechnical Laboratory of the Institute of Technology, Otaniemi
1961/62	Office and Apartment Block, Rovaniemi
1961—64	Opera House in Essen, Germany**
1961—65	Town Hall, Seinäjoki*/**
1961—65	Students' Union of Västmanland-Dala, Uppsala, Sweden**
1962	Group of Apartment Blocks, Tapiola
1962	Enskilda-Bank Building, Stockholm, Competition, 2nd Prize
1962	Cultural Centre, Leverkusen, Germany, Competition**
1962/63	Heating Plant of the Institute of Technology, Otaniemi**
1962/63	Housing Development, Rovaniemi
1962—64	Administration Building of the Scandinavian Bank, Helsinki**
1962—66	Hotel for Students at Otaniemi**
1962—66	Terraced Housing, Jakobstad
1962—68	Stockmann Department Store, Expansion, Helsinki
1962—68	Scandinavia House, Reykjavik, Iceland**
1962—71	Concert and Convention Hall, Helsinki**
1963	Urban Centre, Rovaniemi**
1963—	Town Plan, Otaniemi
1963—65	Institute of International Education, New York, USA, Interior**
1963—65	Library, Seinäjoki**
1963—65	'Heilig-Geist-Gemeinde' Kindergarten, Wolfsburg, Germany
1963—66	Swimming Hall, Jyväskylä, Extension
1963—66	Student Union Building, Jyväskylä
1963—66	Parish Centre, Seinäjoki**
1963—68	Library, Rovaniemi**
1963—68	Parish Centre in Detmerode, Wolfsburg, Germany**
1964	BP Administrative Building, Hamburg, Germany, Competition, 3rd Prize
1964	Wood Technology Laboratories, Otaniemi
1964—	Administrative and Cultural Centre, Jyväskylä
1964/65	One-Family House, Rovaniemi
1964—66	Urban Design Project for Stensvik
1964—66	Extension to Tuberculosis Sanatorium, Paimio
1964—67	Ekenäs Savings Bank, Tammisaari**
1964—68	Administration Building for the City Electric Co., Helsinki
1964—69	Library of the Institute of Technology, Otaniemi**
1964—70	Sports Institute, University of Jyväskylä
1965	Urban Centre Castrop-Rauxel, Germany, Competition**
1965—68	'Schönbühl' High-Rise Apartment House, Lucerne, Switzerland**
1965—70	Library of the Mount Angel Benedictine College, Mount Angel, Oregon, USA**
1966	Experimental Town, Gammelbacka, Porvoo

1966	Housing Development in Pavia, Italy**
1966	Cultural Centre, Siena, Italy**
1966	Theatre in Wolfsburg, Germany, Competition, 2nd Prize**
1966	Riola Parish Centre, Bologna, Italy**
1966	Prototype for Administration Building and Warehouse of the Societa Ferrero, Turin, Italy
1966—69	Academic Bookshop, Helsinki**
1966—69	Town Hall, Alajärvi
1967	Protestant Parish Centre, Zürich-Altstetten, Competition, 1st Prize**
1967—69	Kokkonen House, near Helsinki
1968—	Theatre, Seinäjoki**
1968—71	Water Tower of the Institute of Technology, Otaniemi
1969—	Dwellings with restaurant at the lake, Lucerne, Switzerland
1969/70	Villa Schildt, Tammisaari
1969/70	Parish Centre, Alajärvi
1969—73	Art Museum Aalborg, Denmark
1970	Church in Lahti (revised plan)**
1970	Art Gallery in Shiraz, Iran**
1970	Theatre, Alajärvi
1972—	Theatre, Rovaniemi
1973	Convention Hall, Helsinki, Expansion

Works marked with asterisks are described in greater detail in the comprehensive survey of the architect's work published by Artemis Verlag; a single asterisk refers to Volume I (1962) and a double asterisk to Volume II (1971), from which this book has been adapted.

Photographic Sources

Morley Baer, Berkeley; Rolf Dahlström, Helsinki; Karl Fleig, Zürich; Robert Gnat, Zürich; Peter Grünert, Zürich; Heikki Havas, Helsinki; H. Heidersberger, Wolfsburg; Holmström, Ekenäs; Kalevi Hujanen OY, Helsinki; H. Iffland, Helsinki; Eva und Pertti Ingervo, Helsinki; Peter Kaiser, Zürich; Mikko Karjanoja; Kleine-Tebbe, Bremen; Pekka Laurila, Helsinki; Wolf Lücking, Berlin; Mats Wibe Lund, Reykjavik; Eino Mäkinen, Helsinki; Kalevi A. Mäkinen, Seinäjoki; Leonardo Mosso, Turin; O. Pfeiffer, Lucerne; Pietinen, Seinäjoki; István Rácz, Helsinki; Simo Rista, Helsinki; Roose, Helsinki Matti Saanio, Rovaniemi; Lisbeth Sachs, Zürich; Ezra Stoller, New York; Karl und Helma Toelle, Berlin-Lichterfelde; Valokuva Oy., Kolmio; Gustav Velin, Turku.